MONEY:
Yours, mine or ours?

by
Jason Deane

PublishNation
www.publishnation.co.uk

For Clare, Jed and Anya.
It's all for you, now and always.

Foreword

What this book is … and what it isn't

There are many excellent books on the abstract concept of money management, but there are very few which give you the *exact* tools and *exact* instructions to make the difference. This one will. It even comes with free copies of the pre-programmed spreadsheets used throughout this book if you want them.

This book is designed specifically to help couples in a long term committed relationship, whether married or not and with children or not, get on the same page concerning home budgets, personal spending and financial goals. Too often, money is a source of conflict but, as we'll see, it really doesn't have to be.

By following the steps in this book and putting in some initial work, you will create a clear way ahead and gain total clarity on what it is you want to achieve. Ideally, both partners should read it and work together, but it's not unusual for one or the other to take the lead initially and drive the changes required.

It's not, however, designed to be a Utopian solution to everything in a relationship (although removing financial friction always has a beneficial effect!), nor does it specifically deal with wealth generation beyond your current sources of income. This is about creating a solid foundation and getting the main principles right - in real and precise practical terms rather than fluffy concepts – before you embark on your next financial adventure.

So, whether you have some seemingly impossible hurdles that appear to be blocking your way such as worries about debt or being stuck at a total financial impasse with your partner, or even if you just want to get a better budgeting process in place for your family, this book - and it's proven system - will help you get that balance right.

Enjoy your journey – it has already begun!

Introduction

Although I am not a financial advisor in any capacity, I discovered early on I had a natural ability to manage money.

Even as a teenager and student, I noticed I did things that other people didn't, such as logging expenditure, tracking bank accounts, forecasting where shortfalls were going to occur and so on. As life moved on and complexities inevitably crept in, I devised a system based around my own personal financial goals that worked whilst still ensuring that my monthly commitments were always met. While my friends were spending money because it was simply in their bank account (forgetting that the rent was coming out in a few days), I was staying within my limits and pro-actively dealing with shortfalls. It must be said that I was never wealthy during that time, but I always met my commitments - although it sometimes meant a lean month for social spending.

Over time, I honed the system and developed it with my partner into what it is today. Of course the complexity levels continued to grow as life moved on, particularly when children were added into the mix, but our system now allows us to achieve the following:

- Work towards shared (and mutually agreed) financial goals
- Manage our money on a day to day basis with minimal input
- Clear any debts whilst still being ready for nasty surprises
- Keep us both aware of what exactly our monthly limits are and ensure our spend remains within them
- Give us both some independence to make our own money decisions, whilst knowing that all our commitments are being met

Then, quite a few years ago now, I got a phone call from a family member to help them with their finances. After one look, it was clear there was no control in place, the stress at home was immense and the situation was pretty desperate. A few evenings' work and a copy of the spreadsheets later, we'd reduced their bills by hundreds a month, created a buffer for unexpected spending and given both partners clarity. They worked hard at the system and, over time, it paid off in dividends.

This was followed by more phone calls, more evenings spent with other couples, then friends, then friends of friends and so on. Each situation was mired by its own complexities, but in each case the system worked. I never charged for my time but I did get great satisfaction from watching the stress drain away and learning more and more about the hidden workings of every couple's financial issues that were different from my own and finding similarities that existed between them. More than once the comment "You should write a book!" was raised and here, although somewhat later than planned, is the result.

And *my* financial situation? Let's just say my own financial story has been one of highs and lows. Being a natural risk taker, I have been what many would consider to be 'well off' when things have gone well and I have endured extended periods of being on the breadline when they haven't. But through every twist and turn, I have managed to retain control of the home and personal budgets and work through it by ensuring that the framework I'd created stayed in place and the commitments were met. I have probably made every mistake there is, some of them more than once (just to double check they really were actually mistakes), but the point is that the system you are about to adopt is entirely proven and I have thoroughly crash tested it – personally and via many other couples that I've worked with - through all manner of scenarios.

Once you have clarity, control and balance in place, you'll have a solid foundation on which to move on to the next part of your financial journey with confidence and understanding. It really is a liberating experience!

I should state there's a bit of work ahead, but we'll go through it step by step and I'll explain everything in detail. Remember also that the examples I give are just that – examples. The numbers shown may not be in any way relevant to your own situation, but as you'll see that doesn't matter at all in the end, just the application of the methods themselves.

This book is really aimed at couples who are in a committed relationship (either married or not) and on relatively fixed incomes, i.e. perhaps work for a salary each month. In terms of what you'll learn and apply, it doesn't matter if you do or don't have children, as it will also work for larger families. All the principles can be applied if one or both of you are self-employed, although there are some extra variations and considerations to deal with which I don't propose to cover in detail here (such as tax, dealing with extreme fluctuations in income etc)

This book will help you even if you're in serious debt, have absolutely no idea what state your finances are really in, have limited or no understanding of how money really works, or simply want to plan for a stress free future. The fact is, the timeless principles covered, which I will show you how to apply to the real environment in detail, deal with all these issues and, even better, it's much simpler than you think. All it requires is some initial effort, an ongoing commitment to stay on track and an understanding of basic maths.

Above all, as you complete each step, know that you are taking control as you do so. You are probably no more than a few hours away from getting total clarity and balance ....

... so let's get started!

Chapter One
Get your head right

You're about to face a task that you may consider daunting, overwhelming or even - in your mind - impossible. Perhaps you're only half-heartedly reading this because you think your circumstances are too unique, or your situation is too far gone to recover from. Perhaps you're so stressed about the whole thing, you just can't take it in.

If some, or all, of this applies to you, then this chapter will probably be the most important one in the book. Before we start directly tackling the problem, we need to stare into the abyss and not be afraid. To do this we need to deal with the stress that comes with money being in control of your actions, the distractions that it inevitably leads to and the lack of clarity and focus that results from the previous two. After all, if you're sitting there with a belief that the situation is so hopeless this book can't possibly help, the chances are that you won't be inspired enough to do anything about it. This is dangerous because ultimately the situation WILL change, it's just a question of whether you control and manage that change or external forces, such as being in a situation where you just can't pay the bills any more, forces that change on its own terms.

Equally, of course, you might already have some knowledge about what you're doing and simply want to improve things, in which case you may already know some of what lies ahead. However, as I mentioned in the introduction, we're going to start from the beginning so that you have an entire solution at your fingertips and you can simply take away the bits you need. So let's begin.

First, let's deal with this deep held belief, if it applies, that the situation is so bad nothing can help. Let me ask you a question:

What if your belief is wrong?

Take a second here to think about this simple premise. We change our minds sometimes, we change our opinions and we change our views quite regularly based on new information we get, but we almost never change our beliefs. A belief is a strong, almost unshakeable, association we create with information that we give an unqualified acceptance to. But what if that information that created the belief in the first place isn't right? What happens then? The simple answer is that it gives us the opportunity to challenge and change that belief.

As already alluded to, my own financial journey has been one of extremes at times. My 'bad times' have been VERY bad times. I have personally faced incredibly difficult periods of uncertainty and even stared bankruptcy in the face. I have found myself in situations where I have been liable for enormous debts where a business has failed, with the phone ringing and burly gentlemen knocking at the door. I felt as if I'd strapped myself into a fairground ride from hell that I had initiated but had absolutely no control over. I no longer even had the confidence to speak to people about it and withdrew from the world and my family, often avoiding phone calls and putting the post straight in the bin. Surely, with a situation this bad, nothing could save me. This, of course, was a simple belief. And it was wrong.

In the end I took enough brave decisions to fix it, but it took time and it took effort to overcome my own doubts and we'll learn more about this later. But it also meant letting go of this idea that I couldn't do anything about it, because the fact is that you always, always can. Sometimes, however, the way through is so far hidden, it may as well be impossible to find. But help is at hand and we can find it together.

Dealing with this untrue belief is not easy, and it may take you some time – it certainly did for me. For now, I would ask you to just to trust me on this and let me take on the burden of responsibility for any consequences that may arise if I turn out to be wrong. You'll learn later why I say that with so much confidence.

This is all very well, but now we have to deal with the pressures that come from being in a difficult financial situation. The chances are that you're worrying about it all the time and it's eating away at your confidence. Perhaps you're grumpier than you used to be, you can't sleep at night, or you struggle to get up in the morning as you're dreading what the day ahead may bring. You might suddenly find that you have a short fuse with family and friends or you've become preoccupied and distant. These are some of the many symptoms of stress and you may well recognise them.

We have to deal with this before we can move on and so we shall, right now.

Stress is defined in a number of different ways, but the simplest definition is usually best and this fits the bill superbly in my view:

Stress is caused by not being in control

Yes, it's another obvious statement once you read it. Even better, we can test it, right here, right now to prove how true it is. It's essential you do this part if you're this way, because it's a very simple exercise with powerful and immediate results. It will open your mind very quickly and give you a glimpse of what life will be like when you get this monkey off your back. Are you ready?

Find somewhere quiet and get into a comfortable position, preferably where you can close your eyes for a moment. If you're the sort of person who worries what other people might think about you doing this, find somewhere private so your brain won't interrupt you with thoughts of 'I wonder what they're thinking?'

Imagine now you've won the lottery. But before you get too excited, imagine this was a special lottery that ONLY paid off all your debt. You still have to earn your living and you still have all the ongoing responsibilities such as rent or mortgage (only any arrears would be cleared), power, rates etc. but all your past mistakes would be immediately and unequivocally forgiven. Your income would now go to you and your family rather than creditors, and you'd be given a complete second chance. What would you do differently this time round with your money? The same again? Or would you make some changes and keep control? More to the point, can you imagine actually having the choice? For the moment, forget material things like a better car, house or furniture, focus only on how that would *feel* to have the choice. Does it bring a smile to your face?

If you've never seen it, take a bit of time out to watch the film 'Click' with Adam Sandler. It's a comedy that delivers a powerful message in a warm and comedic way, about a man so wrapped up in the detail of life including, amongst other things, the pursuit of money and a better career, that he neglects the things that are important to him. At the end of the film when he is faced with the reality of where his decisions have taken him as an old man on his deathbed, he is given a second chance. Needless to say, this time round his approach is entirely different. What about you? What would YOU do differently? Winning this magic lottery gives you, to an extent, a second chance. But here's the great bit: it's not a lottery. Anyone can do this with some focus and effort. And that – most definitely - includes you.

When you were imaging yourself in this magic lottery winning situation, I'm sure you'll agree that it was a totally different feeling to the one you're experiencing at the moment. Yet, you've still got to earn your living and you still have the same responsibilities, so what's actually changed? As you've probably guessed, control has now shifted solely to you. It is you, and you alone, who chooses where the money goes.

Now that we have identified what causes this horrible, lingering feeling that follows you wherever you go, we can deal with it. Not in a fluffy, vague way, but by using real, practical tools that can be directly applied to work on your situation on a timescale that suits you. In short, you will start to feel less stress the moment you implement the first step, and by the time we have finished you will be in full control, with that stress being a distant memory.

7

There's just a couple more important mental notes to make before we tackle the maths, paperwork and reality step by step. The first is a concept that will help start liberating you from any anxiety and stress right from the get go. It's not even a secret. It's obvious. Are you ready for this?

Always remember, it's just money.

That's it. It's that simple. Money is just pieces of paper, bits of metal and numbers on a screen. It's meaningless until we attach meaning to it. That meaning could be positive, such as the ways and means to purchase something and provide security or freedom, or it could be a constant source of stress, anxiety or arguments in the home. The truth is, most of us probably recognise the latter scenario more than the first.

So, our first step is to dissociate ourselves from the emotional attachment we have to it. It may be easier said than done, but the concept IS simple. This is incredibly important as we'll see later, because our emotional attachment causes us to make all sorts of utterly mad money decisions driven by greed, love, insecurity, impulse, the desire to impress and so on. We almost never think of it as a mere tool to achieve what we want in life. But it is, and that's all it is.

One of my favourite anecdotes about understanding the importance of money in the grand scheme of things is a hypothetical story about what you would do in a certain situation. It goes like this:

Imagine you're at the top of a very tall building. There is a sheer drop and certain death below you if you fell. Now imagine there's a second building of a similar height a couple of hundred feet away and a long plank of wood is resting on the roofs of those buildings connecting the two. It's raining, the plank is wet, and the wind comes in sudden gusts so strong they could blow a man over in an instant. Let's say I'm on the other building, facing each other at each end of that plank, and I'm holding a suitcase. I open the suitcase and there's £100 in it. You can have it if you cross over to me and get it via that plank of wood. Would you cross? No way. What about if I added a zero, so that it was £1,000? Still not tempted? Well, let's call it a cool million then, how about now?

Of course, crossing the plank is a ridiculous thing to do and very risky. You might make it, you might not, either way the consequences are serious. But you always have the option to walk away, and most people probably would, even if they thought about it for a bit (and perhaps tested how sturdy the plank was first!)

Now let's take it a step further and down a darker path. Imagine instead of the suitcase, I have your children in my arms (if you don't have children, imagine your loved one in the same predicament.) This time, you're not crossing for money, you're crossing to save their lives. Would you do it then? Chances are you'd be on that plank and in my face before I'd even finished the sentence, yet the risks haven't changed, have they? They've simply become irrelevant to what is as stake. Money can never, ever do that. So whilst we focus on improving our situation, remember what is ultimately important and that money is no more than a simple tool. Yes, it must be respected, but it does not control you and it does not call the shots. Unless you let it.

Don't worry if takes a bit of time for you to get your head round this concept, because it could be that you're as sure as hell feeling pretty emotional about it right now. The fact is, it will probably take some time because we're undoing years and years of thinking this way. For now though, if you can simply trust me that this will ultimately help you and then follow the rest of the principles in this book, that's good enough for me. The tools that follow will get you there naturally.

Finally, before we move on to the practical side of this journey, there's one more question I'd like you to ask yourself:

Who controls your thinking and decisions – you or your money?

Most people stop and think before answering this question simply because it's not one they've thought about before. It might also not be immediately obvious until we qualify it a bit, so let me be more precise with a few examples that illustrate the point quite nicely:

When you go out for a drink with your partner in the evening, or a meal with your family, do you ever worry about whether you can really afford it?

Have you ever gotten nervous as you've approached the counter at the grocery store about whether your card will be declined or not? Then, felt a huge relief as it goes through?

Have you ever had some bad news about the car, perhaps a failed MOT, and could *only* think about the money involved?

These are all classic indications of how much money affects our thinking and I'm sure you can think of hundreds of other situations from your own experience. We've all been there at some point or another!

Now think about this scenario:

Your best friend calls. He's getting married. He wants you to be his best man at his wedding, and also to organise the stag do. He wants to go abroad for a couple of days and have a blast.

What's your first thought?

Perhaps it's 'fantastic!' or 'good for him! I knew they'd make a great couple'. Perhaps it's more like 'How the hell am I going to pay for all this?' If you're in the latter camp then you are not in control of your money. IT is in control of you, and your thought processes. Can you even dare to imagine how great it would be never to have that thought cross your mind?

It IS possible. It's all about you being in control, and remembering money is no more than a simple tool. It's amazing to think that very few people fully understand that and even less actually take action to move themselves into a position of control. If you're still not convinced, just listen to comments your friends make in social situations; how often does money, or lack of it, come into the conversation in any format? Now that you're aware of it, you'll spot that it happens all the time. The simple reality is that 95% the population never get any real control of their money and spend their whole lives chasing the next dollar to pay the bills. It's no way to live. Perhaps you already know what I mean.

I should mention that control of money and using it correctly is absolutely nothing to do with how much you earn. Earning is only part of the equation because to one extent or another we can all do that, the real skill is controlling that money and, as we've seen, if you don't, it sure as hell is going to control YOU.

Again, we can illustrate this point with some examples. If you're currently earning £25,000 a year, do you think you'd be happy and have no money worries if you earned £50,000 a year? If you're already earning that £50,000 and yet still struggling from time to time, would £200,000 be the level that brings you a stress free existence? Maybe. My experience, however, tells me it doesn't make much difference what you earn if you have no control or balance in place. The problem is that we all have a tendency to spend to the level we're earning, don't we? We'll stretch the budget to get the biggest mortgage we can (we almost never consider property BELOW what our limit is do we?), we'll buy the best car we can (rather than the one perhaps, we actually need) and so on.

Remember your first paycheques? Could you survive on them now? Probably not, but at the time it was all the money in the world, wasn't it? So what happened? The answer is partly that things change and life happens, but, as we've seen, the other big part of this is who is in control of what you earn – and it may not be you. At this point it no longer matters though, because we're about to take control. For good.

<u>Chapter Two</u>
Getting your partner on board

Whether you're relationship is quite new or you've been together for some time, chances are your finances will be linked somehow.

Perhaps you have a joint account. Perhaps you share a certain amount of money into each other's accounts depending on who the main breadwinner is. Perhaps you have children together or one of you might have other children you are financially responsible for. Perhaps the house is only in your partner's name, but you both pay for its upkeep. There are an infinite number of possibilities in this day and age, but all that matters here is simplifying what we're doing and coming up with an agreed and common way forward.

In some cases, both parts of the couple will be working together and that's great if you're there as it will make moving forward reasonably straightforward and much of this section may not apply to you. However, I've created a whole chapter on this subject because a) this is not always the case and it's critically important that you <u>are</u> on the same page and b) money *can* be a very touchy subject between couples, often leading to arguments and misunderstandings.

First, be aware that you're not alone, this is very common. Many surveys have been carried out over the years and the numbers vary depending on the exact question asked, but it is clear by any measure that couples do not communicate well about money in general. In almost every case, this is either because there is a lack of financial control in the household, there are polar opposite views on what is and isn't important or there is a general feeling that there isn't enough available for the requirements of the family or couple in the first place.

The symptoms of this are typically as follows:

Resentment:

"He/she won't let me spend x on y, but he/she spent a on b"

Disagreement:

"I think *this* is more important than *that*"

Secrecy:

"Don't tell the wife/husband/partner but I spent x on y"

Of course, there are many other manifestations of this discord, but these tend to be the most common. Ultimately they all tend to lead to the same place and it's not a good one. But we can also be forgiven because almost none of us have any training on managing money and we tend to have wildly different personal goals, even where they may involve our partners. Mainly, however, it's because there is always a finite amount of the stuff. Have you ever overheard a couple arguing over having *too much* money? Probably not.

Fortunately, the truth is that as long as your relationship is basically solid, you can, together, overcome anything, including this everyday issue. The key, as always, is open and honest communication. As clichéd as it sounds, that's a hard fact.

The first thing to do is set aside a time without distractions (such as kids, family, work, television, phone calls etc.) where you can get the whole thing in the open. My partner and I laughingly refer to these as 'board meetings' which is closer to the truth than you may at first think. All companies have board meetings to manage the business, money and strategy and this is not that different. Where there's money involved and decisions to be made on everything from the mundane expenditures to the big long term plans, you must both be clear where you're going and how to manage it. Not that different is it?

If you haven't done this before, it may be an eye opening and liberating experience, tinged with some relief and even excitement of what lays ahead. On the other hand, it may also be something that both or one of you fear like nothing else with thoughts of conflict, accusations and long silences. If it's the latter scenario then it's even more important that this happens before the situation deteriorates as it inevitably will.

13

My partner and I have even had 'board meetings' over a meal in a restaurant without the kids to make decisions on things that are coming up. We've had some funny looks sometimes if we're sitting there with some paperwork, but it's a great environment to focus the mind and it works for us. It may for you, or you may prefer something a little more private.

Here are some basic do's and don'ts to get you started:

DO listen to the other person, even, inevitably, when you want to butt in and defend your position or belief. Let him or her finish and ask questions so that you can fully understand where he or she is coming from.

DON'T accuse, belittle or get confrontational about any issues. The past is absolutely and entirely not relevant here, only the future. Chances are you've both done something wrong financially at some stage, because everyone has.

DO stay focussed on the subject at hand.

DON'T get emotional or try and bring other issues into the discussion. Money couldn't care less about your emotional position. It's just a tool waiting for you to use it correctly.

This is not always easy. We are human, imperfect and usually passionate about this subject. This is all about finding common ground, discovering any issues, and, at this point, agreeing only to move forward together. The detail comes later and it's likely to be far, far easier to deal with if you get the basic framework right as we'll see later on.

The ultimate goal for this meeting is for both of you to agree to be totally honest and transparent going forward and to work together to get control and balance.

That's it. That's all you need at this stage. If you can achieve this, you're in good shape to move forward as a solid team. You will need a few more board meetings in due course as we go through various sections, each dealing with specific issues, but in truth this one is the most important of all.

In my experience, it is usual for one partner to take the lead, do the work that follows in this book and present the findings to the other. This is perfectly fine because this agreement still requires that you both remain open and honest at all times. Even better, if you think you can do it together, this is a great step forward because you will almost certainly find that it brings you closer as a natural by-product of carrying out the exercise. In any case, simply remember that you'll both be in a far better position at the end than you were when you first started.

I also have to add a word of warning because the reality is that this is a classic 'carrot and stick' situation. If you can't agree, this whole thing is not likely to work well, so the simple truth is that you need to revisit this until you can. This may require a stark examination of the consequences of *not* working together.

Consider the following:

If you have kids, you need to be the example to them. This includes how you treat each other on this subject. They will do what you do, not what you say, and will use you as their points of reference, either positively or negatively, as they go through their own lives.

If you're struggling financially, or not achieving your goals as a couple or as an individual, then understand this will continue, as true as I type these words, until the situation changes. That is, the situation forces change or you both agree to change your situation. The difference between these two is vast.

If you're doing OK financially but are still finding yourself disagreeing with your partner on issues concerning money, then this also will not change until you both agree to work together.

These are just some of the things you must bear in mind when having this discussion, but if you doubt the importance of having it, just remember the old adage:

If you want to change some things in your life, then you have to change some things in your life.

That change, fortunately, is within your control, even if you don't see it right now. It always, always is.

Most importantly, you must remember what it is you're trying to achieve here. Once you have worked together, followed the steps in this book, and installed the systems I'll show you, you will both have a very clear understanding of where you are going. You'll also both have some independence from each other in terms of what you want to spend 'your' money on (this is key and is dealt with in some detail later) as well as the interdependence that will always exist. Best of all, you will both have peace of mind that every day you're moving forwards, not backwards. Trust me, it's a wonderful, liberating experience and even if there may be some bumps, even crashes, on the way, it WILL be worth it. That, I promise you.

Finally, as you've probably observed, this can naturally lead to a very big area of discussion as it touches on what your goals are as a couple, where you see yourselves in a few years' time and what you want your relationship to be, all of which are far beyond the scope of this book. If this discussion starts leading onto these other things, it's actually a positive outcome and you're likely to have some wonderful and exciting board meetings in the future. There are many excellent books out there concerning goal setting, building relationships and understanding each other and I've listed, on my website, a few of the ones that I would recommend if you're interested in this area. To see the list, simply go to www.originalcrypotoguy.com, select 'Books by Jason' and the title of this book.

But for now, let's get this money issue sorted out. Together.

Chapter Three
Sort it out

So where we do we start? The truth is that everyone is different. Some people keep all their records neatly in coloured, labelled folders in chronological order, some people have 'piles' where they roughly know where things are, some have a big box of 'stuff' and still others haven't got a clue where the hell *anything* is. For the purposes of covering all the bases, we're going to start right at the beginning and when we get to the point where you recognise yourself to be, start taking action from there.

Before we can start sifting through the chaos that may be, we must make order from it. We MUST know exactly what we're dealing with and exactly what the relevant numbers are. If you try and skip this part, the rest of this will not work and you will not deal with the fundamental issues that are causing the problem. So, our first exercise is to tackle that ominous and rather scary pile of paperwork that's been taunting you from the corner of the room, and haunting you mentally at night. Do not, I implore you, go beyond this chapter without completing all the actions in this chapter, fully and completely, first.

Over the years I have helped many people start from a point of chaos and create order. The effect is always positive. Sometimes you can actually see the stress levels starting to come down as one of the demons in the mind is slain for good. The truth is, doing something as apparently mundane as sorting out paperwork is a truly liberating experience. Our brains, at one level or another, like order and logic - it's something we can understand. We all know this of course, but it's just that sometimes not sorting something is, well, just easier isn't it? A little thing here, a little thing there and before you know it, it's too much of a mess to get to grips with. Sound familiar?

We'll do this in steps and sections to make it easier. Remember, you can do this in a day, a week or even longer. The timescale is in your control, all that matters is that the objective is achieved before we move on.

Step one:

Find every single piece of paper relating to your finances and stack them in one pile

Now obviously if you're the sort of person who already has all their paperwork in order, you can skip this part and use the following sections simply as a checklist that you have everything you need. If you're not, and you're like many people who just shove it all somewhere, then we need to address it head on.

When I say everything, I mean 'everything'. That bank statement you shoved under the sofa a couple of months ago. That thick wad of dull looking insurance renewal documents that are still in the envelope by the front door. Those crumpled receipts shoved into the glove compartment of the car. Those bills on the fridge. That bunch of generic paperwork that keep getting added to the 'bits n pieces' drawer in the kitchen. Yes, I also mean that pile of paperwork we want to ignore that might have bad financial news in it. Don't forget that these days we spend a lot on line – are there bills and receipts that may also be relevant to us there?

So, once again, I mean EVERYTHING from EVERYWHERE, so search high and low and take your time. Don't worry about what's on it right now, we're not going to be making any decisions at this point, let's just get it in one place.

Get some music on if you like, involve your partner, find a place where it's all going to go and do your detective work. Later we're going to be referring to the numbers on those pieces of paper, so you'll need them all to hand and in some sort of order to make that processes as simple and as painless as possible.

Now we can move on to step two.

Step two:

Sort all the paperwork into what is, and isn't relevant

Think of this as a 'first pass.' Our objective here is to simply reduce the amount of paper we have in front of us, because it could be enormous and we'll may only need some of it. Here's some guidance:

You can get rid of the following:

Bank statements over six years old (you are supposed to keep all records up to six years old in case the Inland Revenue want to have a nose through and check your tax returns.)

Payslips over six years old.

Old **insurance documents**: unless you have a claim pending on previous year's house or car insurance, you don't need old policies, statements and summaries. This also applies to phone insurance, travel insurance etc.

Credit or store card statements: anything over six years old can be binned. If you think you might have a claim for PPI (Payment Protection Insurance), you can go back ten years, so bear that in mind also.

Mortgage/secured loan statements: I always recommend keeping all of these while any loan is still running.

Rates/electricity/gas/water bills: as long as these have been paid, you don't need to keep previous years' bills, unless you need them for tax return purposes (e.g. you're self-employed and you claim a portion for office use at home.)

Rent books: Old ones from previous addresses don't usually need to be kept, but it's always wise to keep any current agreements.

Car documents: You'll need to keep all service documentation as you'll need to present it when you sell your car, but old V11's, fines information and general correspondence is usually fine to dispose of. Purchase information of the vehicle is also worth keeping.

General bills such as phone, internet, TV: in most cases, the current year is all you need to keep, unless, again you're self-employed and can claim any against your business.

Receipts: General shopping, travel and parking receipts don't need to be kept, but for larger items such as white goods, it's usually a good idea to keep for a couple of years in case there's a problem with the unit and you need to make a claim. Again, some of these will be relevant if you are self-employed.

TV license bill: current year only.

Life insurances: All documentation pertaining to current lives insured.

Children's trust funds: Keep all documentation for any account that's running.

Children's bills: Childcare bills etc. may be relevant to keep, and you may have to anyway if you claim any form of Child Tax Credit. Child support information may also be relevant if you're paying support to an ex-partner.

Tax returns and supporting documentation: If you're employed and have no other incomes, you probably don't have to do these, but if you do, the last six years need to be kept.

Anything else: The above list covers all the really critical stuff, but you may find other documents that have financial information in. If you do and you're not sure, best to keep them for the moment, you'll have a better idea of what's relevant later.

This should reduce down your pile somewhat. Remember, this book is primarily aimed at people on a fixed income (ie earn a monthly salary or have a fixed income from savings, annuities or pensions) and if you're self-employed, this list may vary slightly.

When you're disposing of information, please remember that it's likely to contain sensitive information such as name, address, age etc. Thieves and fraudsters have been known to use discarded information to obtain false identities or simply clone them, so don't make it easy for them. If you can, shred any paperwork before putting it in the bin, or burn it if you don't have a shredder.

Finally, if you just can't bear to chuck the information I've mentioned below, by all means archive it if it makes you feel better. You might still want to sort it into categories (see below) but you can just stick them into some labelled envelopes and put them in an archive box in the loft.

Now we have a pile of useful information, we need to get it into order, so we'll move onto step three.

Step Three:

Sort your pile into categories

Although it can be satisfying, no one really enjoys sorting paperwork. This process is about investing the time up front so our interaction with it later is minimal. Trust me on this, it's much, much easier if we stay the course and get this done before we move onto the more interesting stuff.

So now we need to take our pile of paperwork and sort it into categories. After all, it's no good having all the information to hand if we need to go through the whole pile every time we need something from it. This is our second pass and it can still be done reasonably leisurely.

Go through your paperwork and simply create piles of the same documents. So, gas bills with other gas bills, credit card bills with credit card bills and so on. If you have different accounts with the same bank, double check you're putting the right statements together by checking names or account numbers. Again, it's critically important that your partner's details are included if you both have separate bank accounts. Use post it notes on each pile to identify them if you wish.

This may take you some time, and I can't pretend it's exciting, but it's important both from a practical and psychological viewpoint. Just the act of getting that dreaded paperwork in order will start liberating your mind from any stress you may be feeling, I promise you.

You might find that you can reduce your paperwork even further here but you may also end up with a pile of 'miscellaneous' documents that don't fall neatly into any other categories. Don't worry about these at the moment, just keep them all together. We'll soon identify how much information, if anything, we need from this pile in later steps.

Step Four:

Sort your piles of paperwork into date order

Now it's time for the final pass and this time we're going to go through each pile and sort it into date order. Whilst this may seem to be a detail, it makes life considerably easier later on, so it's worth doing. You can go recent first or recent last, whatever you prefer, but make sure that you use the same system throughout to avoid confusion. Bank statements are often numbered and if you find that you're missing some, you may need to find them depending how recent they are. These days, however, it's usually possible to print them off from an online source rather than calling the bank.

Once this chore is done, we need to store them in a way that we can access them easily. Personally, I use a foolscap (i.e. larger than A4) folder in a filing cabinet, sorted by financial year as it makes it easier for any tax returns, but I usually only keep the last three years to hand. Any previous years I'll keep for a while, but they will be archived away from my filing cabinet, which means labelled archive boxes in the loft. Every now and then I'll have a very satisfying clear out of anything that's run its natural course.

The tax year runs from April 6th to April 5th for historical reasons, but for the most part, especially if you're on a fixed income, simplifying it to include April to March is generally acceptable. So, if you have twelve bank statements (one for each month) put them together, bound by a paperclip and a post-it note with the financial year (often abbreviated to 'FY') it refers to. So, if you're dealing with April 2017 to March 2018, you would put 'FY18'. (The year it refers to is always the year where the period ends.)

It goes without saying, of course, we need to form a new habit here. As soon as new paperwork comes in we can add it to the appropriate year in our filing cabinet. This puts you in complete control from now on and also means no piles of crumpled paperwork laying around the house, or madly scrabbling around for a current utility bill if you have to provide proof of address for something. The time you gain will always outweigh the time you have to spend keeping it in order, trust me on this.

Congratulations! You have now completed a major step to taking full control of your finances! Now we need to use the information in these documents to assess where we are and what we need to do to ensure it's YOU who controls where the money goes, and not the other way round. I know it sounds daunting at first, but remember I have used the following system many, many times with people with situations varying from terrifying to excellent and it *always* works. It will work for you too.

So now the foundations are laid, let's take the next, bold steps towards control, balance and peace of mind.

Chapter Four
Assess where you are

Most people don't know what their mortgage payment is (although interestingly most people seem to know what their rent payments are if they are in that situation), when bills are due or even how much they're spending on coffees in the week. For these people, salaries come in and they do the best they can to make it through the month, often falling short and having very little, if anything, to show for their month's work. Sometimes people borrow on credit cards, overdrafts or even pay day loans to make up any shortfall, but this only makes the situation worse. This has another scary side effect, because it gives the illusion that they're able to keep up with life's demands, when they're actually going backwards a little more each month. "After all", we think to ourselves, "everyone has debt, right?!"

Ultimately, if this is not dealt with, they will become another statistic on the personal insolvencies register with potentially devastating and long lasting consequences for them and any dependants. If you recognise any of the above statements, we must take action *now*. But if you're reading this, you already are.

As with any project, before we can achieve our end goal, we must know exactly where we're starting. It's time to do our initial analysis.

For this, by far and away the best tool is a simple home computer and a spreadsheet program such as Microsoft Excel. If your home PC doesn't have Excel and you're worried about the cost of buying it, there are some excellent and completely free alternatives in OpenOffice or LibreOffice which all do the same things which are easily downloaded and installed. I have added shortcuts to them on my website at www.originalcryptoguy.com (under 'Books by Jason' and then the title of this book) so that you can jump straight to them. If you know how to use spreadsheet programs (and if you can use one, you can use them all) then these next steps will be easier, but even if you don't I have set up all the spreadsheets for you and I'll walk you through them step by step. They are ready for you to download, free, as part of buying this book and we'll be doing that in a moment. They're designed for Excel, but they will work in the other formats just as well.

Whilst you will be able to do everything that follows with minimal spreadsheet knowledge by simply following the instructions and examples given, I do think it's a good idea to learn the basics of spreadsheets either by taking a course or reading one of the many excellent books that are out there on the subject. Using spreadsheets is an essential part of today's society and doing any sort of numeric exercise is far, far easier on a spreadsheet when compared to using pen and paper. I have listed some suggestions of books that may help on my website in the same location mentioned above. Clicking on the links will take you straight to where you can buy them.

However, if you feel you're just not computer literate enough, it is possible to do this entire process on a piece of paper. It takes a little longer and you need to be confident in your maths because any mistakes you make will be duplicated as we build up the picture of your finances, but it can be done. Just take your time, double check your numbers and use different pages to represent the different sheets as we go.

I should mention there are all sorts of specialist money management tools these days varying in price and some are even given away with certain bank accounts. They all have pros and cons, but in my view, the simplest, easiest and most universal tool is the humble spreadsheet. It's up to you, of course, but if you use a different tool you'll need to adapt the processes we go through to fit what you're working with.

To download the sheets you need for this book, simply go to www.originalcryptoguy.com, select 'Books by Jason' and then the title of this book. About half way down the page you will see the link to download the spreadsheet file. Simply do so, then open it and save it where you want it to be kept on the PC.

You should arrive automatically on the section called 'WELCOME', but if not, simply click on the tab labelled 'WELCOME' at the bottom of the page and read the notes there. The only thing you need to enter at this stage is your name and your partner's name where indicated, although it doesn't matter which way round you do this. This is important because this is copied automatically through the spreadsheet and allows you to identify certain things as we go through more easily.

This part is very important: If you're a couple living together, we're going to include ALL the income you both earn in one pot and ALL the expenses to start with. I understand, of course, that there may be different accounts and there may be different responsibilities, but we will get to that later. Right now, we need to assess where you are as a whole and make sure you have a basis from which to work, so we're going to pretend there is only one account and everything goes in and out of that single account. We'll add others later and if you're a couple it's important that you have separate ones anyway for certain things as we'll see.

Now we need to populate (this is a term that basically means 'fill in') our first spreadsheet and the one we're going to use is called the 'Master Account Planner (MAP)'. We're looking for, and giving priority to, our 'fixed' and 'mostly fixed' outgoings for the moment.

Simply click on the tab at the bottom of the page as shown below:

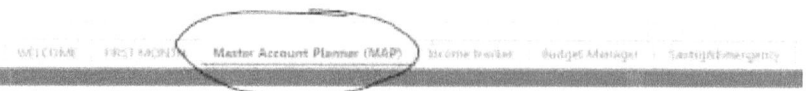

This will bring up the first spreadsheet and you will probably notice that there are already two entries in place, namely 'Personal Allowance for (name of partner one)' and 'Personal Allowance for (name of partner two)' showing as coming out on the first of the month. If you don't see your names there, you may have skipped the

26

first step. Simply return to the 'WELCOME' tab and type in your names where indicated and return to the 'Master Account Planner (MAP)' spreadsheet to carry on from this point.

At the moment, you can safely ignore these 'allowances', but don't (yet) change the monthly amounts from zero, and don't delete them. This is a key part of balancing interdependence and independence which we'll learn more about later.

Now, take your bank statements, those of your partner and any joint accounts you have and start working through them line by line for the last complete month. So, if you're doing this in April, take March's bank statement's first.

In date order, add into the spreadsheet your FIXED and MOSTLY FIXED outgoings first. So, if on the 3rd of the month, your monthly payment for the TV licence comes out (a nice easy fixed payment that doesn't usually change through the year), type '3rd' in the date column, enter 'TV License' under the 'Item Description' column and type in the amount under the 'usual amount' column. Then, do the same for each of the entries on all of the bank statements ignoring for the moment which account it's coming from. We'll simplify bank account management later.

The fixed payments are easy to identify and will not present you with a problem, but we're also looking for payments that are *mostly* fixed. A good example of this would be mobile phone bills or a phone and internet package, where the payment date doesn't change but the amount might vary each month. What to enter here is trickier and this is where access to previous months' data and possibly contracts becomes important from the piles of paperwork we sorted earlier. We'll also include here flexible payments such as credit cards, because, if you're not paying off the full amount each month, chances are your payments vary according to how much you have spare. Later on we'll learn how you'll be dictating what is paid to the card, rather than the other way round, but for now, let's get the data in. Remember, we can tweak these as we learn more about your situation.

A good rule of thumb is that anything that is paid by direct debit or standing order is likely to be either a 'fixed' payment (Standing Orders are by definition 'fixed') or a 'mostly fixed' payment, which means that by the time we've completed this first pass all, or at least the vast majority of, these payments should be included in your spreadsheet.

It's also possible that some 'mostly fixed' payments might be paid by cheque for various reasons, such as credit card payments, but for ease we're going to treat them as if they were done by direct debit for now. Don't worry about this, it's purely for demonstrational purposes as the dates and amounts are what's relevant here rather than the method of payment, and we'll revisit payment mechanisms in due course anyway.

To help you, typical examples of 'mostly fixed' payments are:

- Mobile phone bills
- Landline phone bills (that aren't on fixed payment terms)
- Credit card bills
- Interest charges on things such as overdrafts

And so on.

They'll be all sorts of transactions on the statements of course, especially if you're a prolific debit card user, but at this stage stick strictly to ones that are fixed, or mostly fixed, and tend to repeat each month. Because you're doing it in date order, this should be relatively straightforward and this format will also help you plan ahead as you'll see in due course. If you have more than one payment coming out, say on the 1st of the month, for example, simply add it in under the existing date.

At this point, I'm going to create an imaginary couple with an imaginary financial situation to help us go through this process. This is because it's easier to get used to the spreadsheets if you can see 'real' data being used in them. Our couple, Jim and Alison, have been together ten years, but are not married, and have two young children. Jim works full time and earns around £2,400 a month after tax, Alison works part time and earns around £650. They have life insurance, own their house with an interest only mortgage, two cars (one owned outright, one on a finance plan) and have total debts of around £9,000 in unsecured loans, overdrafts and flexible borrowing (such as credit cards). They receive a small Tax Credit of roughly £100 a month and Child Benefit of roughly £140 a month.

Their jobs allow them to save money on full time childcare as they can stagger their work hours to fit round the children a little, plus, like most people in their situation, Jim's parents take care of the children once a week. Sometimes, childcare is inevitable, but it's not something they pay for on a fixed basis.

I have deliberately chosen a couple with higher than average complexity to demonstrate how the system works, and it could be, of course, that your own situation is more or less complex than this. Remember, it's only an example, and our family doesn't really exist.

Once this process is completed, Jim and Alison have a 'Monthly Account Planner (MAP)' spreadsheet that looks like this:

(Overleaf)

Master Account Planner (MAP)

Expected income (auto fill in from 'Income Tracker' sheet): ➡

Due Out	Item Description	Usual Amount
1st	Personal allowance for Jim	0.00
1st	Personal allowance for Alison	0.00
	TV License	12.12
	Home insurance	28.54
	Water Company	50.18
	TV Package subscription	38.75
5th	Phone insurance company	8.50
	Jim's life insurance	25.00
7th	Child Trust fund	50.00
8th	Credit Card A minimum payment	98.55
12th	Jim's Mobile phone	55.00
	Car Loan repayment	195.00
15th	Gas Company	50.00
	Electricity Company	75.00
18th	Alison's Gym Membership	45.99
19th	Council Tax	144.00
20th	Alison's Life insurance	19.85
22nd	Loan repayment	122.00
	Phone and internet Package	37.50
23rd	Car insurance (combined)	78.00
26th	Mortgage (interest only)	785.00
27th	Alison's Mobile Phone	67.50
	Credit Card B minimum payment	115.50
	Monthly totals	2101.98

It's very important it is in the correct date order as this spreadsheet has several functions which will become clear as we go through. Note that they have grouped any payments that come out on the same day so, for example, the TV License, home insurance, water company and TV Package subscription (as well as the Partner Allowances) all come out on the same day, the 1st of the month.

There's already a couple of things we need to cover. First, notice that they have - correctly - used exact amounts. Many people round the numbers they are using up or down to the nearest whole number, but I always think this is very dangerous because you could still not actually know what the complete picture is after doing the work. If, for example, you have ended up with 25 lines after entering all your information, then you could, in theory, be close to £25 a month out in your Master Account Planner. That's £300 a year we can't account for before we've even started and it's entirely unnecessary. So, if you're going to put the effort in, we may as well get the numbers right.

Second, *some* of these payments aren't paid consistently over the 12 months of the year. Rates bills, for example, are usually over ten months, with a break in February and March. Water rates tend to be paid over nine months, with a break running from December to February inclusive. Don't worry about this at the moment as we'll deal with it later, but you should bear it in mind if you're starting this in one of the months that's affected because it could be that the relevant payment is not on that particular bank statement.

Third, the dates the payments came out of your bank account aren't necessarily the dates that they are due. If the payment to the Gas Co and the Electric Co are due on the 15th as in the example above and the 15th happens to be on a Saturday, it won't come out until the Monday, in this case the 17th. It could even be the 18th if it's a bank holiday. This means it's time to turn detective to confirm the correct dates. You can do this either by looking at previous statements and working out the exact date where it repeats, or logging into the bank accounts online and checking the direct debits/standing orders section of your internet banking. This is worth doing anyway as it acts as a good checklist, but do it this way round so that you're getting to know your statements intimately for the purposes of this exercise.

Finally, even fixed payments, like all others, will change at some point. Rates bills go up annually, mortgage payments could vary with interest rate changes and rents may be negotiated periodically, but the point is that these are fixed for the time being. It's all about being as accurate as possible, but building in the flexibility we'll need as time goes on.

It's very important not to be tempted to try and 'fudge' the numbers by estimating low - you need to be as accurate as possible. If anything, it's always better to estimate slightly higher as this will only help you in the long run.

Don't forget to save your spreadsheet regularly. Because you'll be entering all your sensitive data, it's also a good idea to add password protection. If you'd like to do this but don't know how, simply Google it for the software package you are using and follow the instructions. In all cases, it's quite straightforward.

As you can see looking back at the example, Jim and Alison have a couple of mobile phone bills and some credit cards payments. They've worked out the 'typical' monthly amount by looking back at several bills and working out what's roughly normal, but you could equally take an average. For the credit card payments, they could have taken the amounts they *try* and *usually succeed* to make each month, but instead they opted for typical minimum payments. Either is fine at the moment because we need a starting point to work with that we can fine tune later.

So now we know what our fixed payment schedules are, we know exactly what needs to be in the bank account in cleared funds the day before. It's already a useful tool to have printed out and put on a wall (but away from prying eyes!) somewhere as a reminder.

In our example, Jim and Alison now know that they need £2,101.98 a month to make all their primary payments before they even start looking at miscellaneous expenditure. However, some months will be slightly less due to the variation in when some payments are due. For some people this simple realisation alone can be an eye opener, but this information is critical to getting any future planning right.

You may also notice that there is currently no provision for savings. Don't worry about this yet, as we'll come to that. In the meantime, it's worth remembering that if you have any flexible, unsecured borrowing at all (and I'm really referring to credit cards or overdrafts here) it simply does not mathematically make sense to save money whilst these are still in play. Some people believe this is controversial citing that it is always wise to have a fund available in case of emergencies. Whilst I generally agree with this (and we do actually make a provision for unexpected costs going forward), the fact remains that the amount you earn on savings in *any* savings account will always be less than the amount it costs you to keep a debt running on any credit card. This even applies if you're in an interest free period on your cards because it makes sense to reduce any balance as much as possible before that period ends to avoid the punishing charges that follow. Don't forget, the cards themselves act as a buffer in the event of unforeseen circumstances by their very nature, but in time we're going to wean ourselves off them and find more efficient ways of dealing with unexpected surprises. In short, if you have no credit card debt, or in fact any other kind of debt at all, then ONLY in those circumstances should you be looking at creating an additional savings fund.

This is part one of the account planning process and well done for completing it! Arguably that was the hardest part involving the most effort and research, but we now need to move on to the next stage to get the lay of the land ahead of us.

Chapter Five
Assess what's going out and when

Now that we know our fixed and mostly fixed outgoings, we need to work out what our total monthly commitment will be going forward. Note that we haven't dealt with day to day, one off, leisure or unexpected spend yet, this will all come later. Right now, we have to make sure we're going to be covering everything as and when it's due.

To do this, we're going to complete the rest of the 'Master Account Planner (MAP)' spreadsheet by populating all the figures we know about in each month's column, and in most cases this is relatively simple to do.

Using Jim and Alison's example, they will go through line by line as follows:

Personal allowances: These will be fixed and can be repeated in every month, but we haven't worked out what they'll be yet, so leave at zero for the moment.

TV License: A fixed monthly payment every month of the year, currently £12.12, duplicated across all twelve months

Home insurance: Some home insurance companies spread the payments over 12 months, some 10 and some over completely different periods, so you'll need to check your agreement and schedule. Even if it's a small amount, it's worth doing because several small amounts can make a big difference over time. Jim and Alison pay theirs over ten months, so they will make no payment in June and July.

Water Company: Most, if not all, water companies collect their payments over eight months between April and November inclusive and this applies to Jim and Alison as well, so they simply leave the values for December to March at zero.

34

TV Package subscription: This is an ongoing contract so this will remain the same for the time being across all months.

Phone insurance Company: An annual contract with twelve equal payments, split against each month accordingly.

Life insurance: Whether a 'whole of life' or 'fixed term' policy, monthly payments should be the same. Jim and Alison have insured themselves for a fixed sum for a fixed period and will be paying premiums for another five years, although the premiums come out on different dates.

Child Trust Fund: This is the amount Jim and Alison are paying – via direct debit – into their child's saving or Trust account. They have fixed this so it is the same each month.

Credit Card Minimum Payments: For now, we'll take the first minimum payment and set it at the same for the rest of the year. Of course, the amount should drop slightly every month as the interest gradually reduces, but if we set the same amount it creates a discipline and will clear the debt slightly faster. *IMPORTANT: This only works if you're successful in stopping all spending activity on all credit cards right away.* This system will create a clear framework for you to spend **only** within your means and get total control of your finances. Continuing to use your cards if you have existing balances will make it much, much harder to gain real, full control. Don't worry about this at the moment though, we'll be getting this set up and managed in due course. Right now, you just need to be aware that this is where we want to get to.

Mobile Phone Payments: Even on most fixed contracts there are fluctuations on monthly bills. Create a 'best guess estimate' by, for example, looking at several months and working out an average. It's best to err on the high side (we'll get back any savings later as you'll see) and enter it into all months.

Car loan payment: These will be fixed for the duration of the loan. Jim and Alison's loan is going to finish in October this year when they will own their vehicle outright. They may decide to get another loan for a new vehicle at that point, but they'll decide when they get there as they'll have a very clear picture of both their finances and their goals at that point. For now, they can leave November and December blank.

Gas/Electric Company: These days most people pay a fixed amount by Direct Debit every month and review it once a year. Jim and Alison are no exception and know what their payments are most likely to be until the end of the year.

Alison's Gym Membership: Alison loves swimming and yoga, so often visits the gym when the kids are at school. She is not in a contract, but pays a fixed amount each month to attend.

Council Tax: Usually collected between April and January inclusive, so February and March have no payments showing.

Loan repayment: Jim and Alison took out a loan to refit the kitchen and bathroom two years ago. They are still paying £122 on a fixed term agreement and will be for another 26 months. This will, therefore, remain fixed for the whole period.

Phone & Internet Package: Jim and Alison have a standard landline and internet package which also covers basic TV services. They are in a contract and will be paying this amount until the next price review.

Car Insurance: To take advantage of a deal, Jim and Alison combined their car insurance and pay it at the same time together in one premium each month. It's due a renewal in July, but since they don't know what the premium will be as yet, the monthly figure remains the same for now.

Mortgage: Our couple have an interest only mortgage which still has 14 years to run before the full repayment is due. At the moment, they have no other savings or investments in place to make the full repayment at the end of the term, so they will have to sell the house and downsize. However, they are hoping that by getting their finances in order, they will have the option to avoid this.

Other things: Every couple's situation is different and some careful thinking may be required here. Whilst Jim and Alison have some parental support in terms of looking after the children from time to time, there are some couples who don't have access to this for whatever reason and need to pay for ongoing childcare. In some cases, there may be children from previous relationships that need to be paid in terms of support. There may be extra insurances, private health care or even Christmas savings clubs – all of these need to be considered and added in. Take your time and make sure you've covered every possibility. If however, you later discover something that you missed, the beauty of a dynamic spreadsheet is that you can simply add it in at any time.

Now Jim and Alison have taken the time to work out their payments, which dates they are due and which months they are relevant to, their spreadsheet looks like this:

NOTE: A large, clear version of this image is available at www.originalcryptoguy.com under 'Books by Jason'

Immediately we can see that only in five months of the year is the maximum payment of £2,101.98 due, and they are: April, May, August, September and October. In December, the fixed payments are £245.18 lower, and this isn't unusual for most people in the UK due to the way the bill payments are structured. It's also very handy for Christmas!

Overall, Jim and Alison's position doesn't look too bad now that we can see it in black and white. We already know they have enough income to cover all the fixed payments that they must fulfil each month even before we've looked at the income figures in detail, but they are carrying out this exercise because they still seem to be going backwards and can't work out why. This tells us the problem lies elsewhere and we'll find it as we go through.

Ignore the zero values in the 'Disposable income total' entry for now. Everything is set to zero because we haven't yet carried out the second half of the exercise, the income figures, and this therefore won't be accurate until we have done so.

If, once you have completed this exercise for yourself, you find that you have more money going out than coming in just in terms of fixed payments, don't panic. Take a deep breath, understand that you are dealing with the issue head on right now, and carry on with the next steps so we can clearly understand what we need to do and what the figures tell us. This is EXACTLY the moment you'll probably want to give up if that is the case, but it also EXACTLY the moment that leads to finding that control – just as long as you can get yourself to the end of the process. I can assure you, no matter how bad you think these numbers are, I have seen, dealt with and finally overcome, far, far worse. So, let's take the next step and get a clearer picture.

Chapter Six
Assess what's coming in and when

Now we need to look at our income and we need to do this in the same level of detail we did for outgoings. This is often an interesting exercise and it almost always leads to the discovery of one of the problems people encounter when managing money – that of approximation. In short, if you're not writing down or tracking your income, it can lead to overestimating the amount you have available. If that's the case, then you'll almost always spend more than you should do. The reasons for this are many fold, but the most common is simply the way our brains work. If we receive a combination of weekly, monthly or four weekly payments (as Jim and Alison do), it's very hard to work out what this gives you as a monthly budget, and the frequency of payments gives the illusion that money is always coming in. However, it also blurs the lines between monthly periods which can lead to trouble, so getting a handle on this is critically important.

In a perfect world, all our income coming in and payments going out will be the same, but in practice this never happens. Fortunately, the systems built into the spreadsheets allow you to bring everything to the table and make it visible in a format that makes sense by month. So let's begin, using the same logical system for the income as we did for the outgoings.

Simply click on the 'Income Tracker' tab of the spreadsheet at the bottom of the page, like you did for the previous spreadsheets, and we can start entering the information we need.

We're going to be starting with the fixed income section at the top left of the page. It may look complicated at first, but don't worry because it won't take you long to get used to it. Even better, information that you put here only needs to be entered once as it will be automatically copied through to the other spreadsheets for you. In a moment, we'll be looking at Jim and Alison's entries so we can see how this should look once it's entered.

The spreadsheets are set up so that cells which are greyed out should never be typed in as they usually contain formulas to make the rest of them work. It's a great way to check you are entering your data in the right sections, but if you accidently type in a grey box, simply press the 'undo' button, or restore an earlier saved version.

As before, make sure you save your work every few minutes.

Fixed salary income earned through Pay as You Earn (PAYE)

Most people who work for a company or someone else will fall into this category and Jim and Alison are no exception. This is usually paid net and by calendar month, so it is straightforward. However, if you are paid weekly, bi-weekly or four weekly, you will need to adjust the figures accordingly.

So, if you are paid weekly, the correct formula for working out your monthly income is

Weekly Pay X 52 divided by 12

If it's bi-weekly, it's

Bi-weekly pay X 26 divided by 12

If it's four weekly, it's

Four weekly pay x 13 divided by 12

To make this easier, there is a section on the spreadsheet that does these calculations for you. So, for example, whilst Jim is paid the same amount every calendar month of £2,400, Alison is paid for her part time job every two weeks. This is what the 'Income Tracker' spreadsheet looks like after Jim has entered his income figures:

	A	B	C	D
1	**Income Tracker**			
2		Monthly	Annual	
3	Income source	Amount	Amount	January	Fe
4	*Miscellaneous/bonus/extra income (see below)*			£0.00	£
5	Jim's pay - ACME Co.	2400.00	28800.00	£2,400.00	£2,
6			0.00	£0.00	£
7			0.00	£0.00	£
8			0.00	£0.00	£
9			0.00	£0.00	£
10			0.00	£0.00	£
11			0.00	£0.00	£
12			0.00	£0.00	£
13			0.00	£0.00	£
14			0.00	£0.00	£
15	Total income	2400.00	28800.00	2400.00	24
16	*These figures are automatically added in the Master Acccount Plan*				

You will see that the figures are automatically copied across to the other months going forward. But Alison can't enter her pay in this format because it won't give the correct result, so she needs to convert to a monthly equivalent, either by using the formulas above, or the calculator on the same page.

She chooses the latter and, after looking at her payslips, she works out that she gets £325 every two weeks. She enters this figure into the 'bi-weekly' calculator and gets the following results:

18	Calculator:		
19	**To find monthly incomes, enter figures below:**		
20	Convert annual figure to monthly here:		
21		equals	0.00
22			per month
23	Convert weekly figure to monthly here:		
24		equals	0.00
25			
26	Convert bi-weekly figure to monthly here:		
27	325	equals	704.17
28			per month
29	Convert four weekly figure to monthly here:		
30		equals	0.00
31			per month
32			

Remember when we said that she earns around £650 a month at the start? It turns out it's actually slightly more at £704.17 **ON AVERAGE** per month. She would then enter this number, together with the description of what it is, under Jim's entry done previously.

This is the first time we are taking 'average' figures over 'actual' figures and the reasons for this will become clear later on. For now, understand this is all about 'compartmentalising' the pay period into a nice, neat and easy-to-understand calendar month. Our brains like order and finite time scales, rather than the open ended system most of us tend to run when we're not budgeting correctly. By creating the habit of putting everything into a monthly space, you will have complete control over every penny without having to worry about whether you have enough for the next fixed payment or unexpected bill.

Remember to ONLY put the net figures from the paycheques into the spreadsheets. If you include the gross figures (i.e. including tax, national insurance and any other deductions you may get), your spreadsheet will be entirely inaccurate.

Flexible salary income earned through PAYE

This is typical of part time work, shift work or work that involves bonuses. Things get more complicated here, but we need to come up with a monthly figure even if some months you earn more, or less, than this. Again, this is where research comes in. Look at previous payslips over a period of, say, six months - what was the average? Then ask, was that a typical six months? If yes, then you have your number. If not, then, why was it not typical? What skewed it? Can you remove whatever is making the numbers seem unrealistic and come up with a better number that way?

This is a starting point and we just need an average here to get the ball rolling, so we have something to copy across the rest of the year. If you know that your monthly income will vary each month and this seems at odds with that, don't worry, we'll be able to change the monthly amounts as we go, which we'll learn about later on.

If you have a fixed bonus you may want to include it in the month it is appropriate. For example, Jim's company pay a nominal £100 Christmas bonus each year, so he will set the rest of the year as a fixed income and put the bonus figure in the December income. He does this because it's in his contract and is almost certainly entitled to it. Where performance related bonuses are not in your control, it's usually better to leave them out and add them in if and when they come in.

Jim won't enter the bonus at this stage though, he will add that later when we get to that section.

Child benefit

This is usually paid four weekly, so use the calculations above. This is important because four weeks is NOT the same as a month, as we have already seen in the two week example, and you will end up with an error if you try and apply it that way. Jim and Alison receive £140 every four weeks so, using the calculator, they work out that this is equivalent to £151.67 a month and enter it on the spreadsheet.

43

Tax credits

There are a whole series of tax credits paid by the government to families earning less than around £40,000 a year, although tax credits at the higher end are very small. It's worth checking out if you qualify by checking the appropriate government website. These can be paid weekly or monthly and are usually set at the start of the tax year so are relatively fixed. Our couple receive a small tax credit of around £23 a week. Using the calculator, Alison works out that they get £99.67 a month on average and enters that figure into the spreadsheet.

NOTE: in reality, it's unlikely that Jim and Alison would qualify for any tax credits, but for the purposes of this example and just to show different income types, let's assume they do. They would probably receive the full amount, or very close to the full amount, of child benefit under the current (2018) guidelines.

Anything else

You may have other incomes such as interest on savings, investments, pensions, dividends etc. If so, you need to provide a monthly figure. If you have an income source that is paid only once a year, it is usually better to put that payment in the month that it falls in the 'Miscellaneous Income' area that we'll look at in a moment.

Jim and Alison currently have no savings at all, so this section is not relevant to them as there are no investment or interest payments due.

I need to mention the dreaded 'T' word here – TAX. Extra incomes may well be subject to income tax and your prevailing rate and you must legally declare this income and pay any taxes at the end of each year. For most people on a fixed income, tax is taken care of at source through Pay As You Earn (PAYE) so for the sake of simplicity, I will leave any potential tax payments out for the moment. Certain monies that you receive are not classed as taxable directly, although they may be counted as part of your overall income. These can include things such as family gifts up to a certain amount, premium bond winnings and inheritances (after the estate has paid the inheritance tax), but for a full breakdown, it's worth looking at the HMRC website if you're not sure. Other incomes, for example where you've done a car boot sale or sold an item from your home (that is not part of a business), are frankly, nothing to do with HMRC as they are cash conversions of something you already own.

By the way, it's perfectly fine to minimise your tax bill by any legal means possible – and HMRC expect you to take the responsibility to do that – but it is never wise to avoid paying it altogether where you know it is due.

Jim and Alison have now worked out all their fixed monthly incomes, and their spreadsheet now looks like this:

NOTE: A larger, clearer version of this image is available at www.originalcryptoguy.com under 'Books by Jason'

The fixed incomes have been added across all the months and we can see, on average, the couple receive £3,355.51 a month in salaries, child benefit and tax credits over the year. This is actually well above the national average for household income and they should be living quite comfortably, yet somehow they are not able to make ends meet.

45

It looks like we'll need to do further analysis going forward to find where the issue is.

Before we do that, however, we need to work out if there are any other incomes that we know about for the year.

Ad-hoc or miscellaneous income

Jim has already identified that he will get a bonus of £100 in December. Alison thinks she is going to have a big clear out of the garage later in the year and sell off a load of stuff via eBay or car boot sales, but she can't say for sure what those incomes will be right now, so she can't include them as yet. For now, therefore, Jim simply adds his £100 bonus into the 'Misc. income' section in the space reserved for December's income. Note that this is then automatically included in the total income for the month, which is then fed into the other spreadsheets.

Jim likes to be organised, so he adds a note on the spreadsheet by right clicking on the cell he has entered the £100.00 bonus in and selecting 'add comment'. He then types in 'Christmas bonus' so that if he ever needs to know what it is, he can simply roll the mouse over the cell and be reminded.

The figures, the ones that we know about anyway, are now complete for the year, but there is yet another positive side effect of setting things up this way. Effectively, if you were to generate extra income over the year, the impact on your budgets and leisure spending is easily measured and accounted for. This creates an extra psychological benefit because it gives you a real incentive to bring in that extra money because anything you generate will not now be 'lost' in the noise of a poorly managed budget. Instead it can be put to work immediately in any way you see fit.

We'll cover more on this later, but for now let me plant the seed of thinking about your couple's financial set up as a 'business'. Even if you have never run a business in your life and the thought of it absolutely terrifies you, I'm here to tell you that you're already

46

running one. You're dealing with quite a lot of money over the period of a year, and having to manage the outgoings inevitably incurred as a result of running the business of living. And, like any business, it's all about getting the balance right, and not just financially, though that is the focus of this book.

Your 'company's cash flow' is subject to unexpected problems, or even the occasional surprise, but your earnings and lifestyle are not necessarily limited even if you're on a fixed income. At the end of the day, it's all about making a few decisions to make sure it is YOU who is in control and not the money that you're working for.

So, with that thought in mind, let's move on to the next stage and have a look at our day to day expenditure.

Chapter Seven
Daily spend – where's the money going?

This part of the spreadsheet system we're only going to use once, because we need to work out where you are and how you got to that point. Basically, it's a bit of analysis that is essential to set us up going forward, but we don't necessarily need to go back to it – except to look back and smile in years to come!

For this section, we simply need to click on the 'FIRST MONTH' tab back at the bottom of the screen in the same way as we have done before to access the other spreadsheets.

To begin with, we need to work out which month we're going to be using. So, if you're getting your finances together in April, you'd select March as your first month to analyse in detail. It doesn't really matter where you are in the month, but if you're right at the end of it, i.e. the last couple of days, you might want to do the one you're in and finish it off as the last bits of information come in.

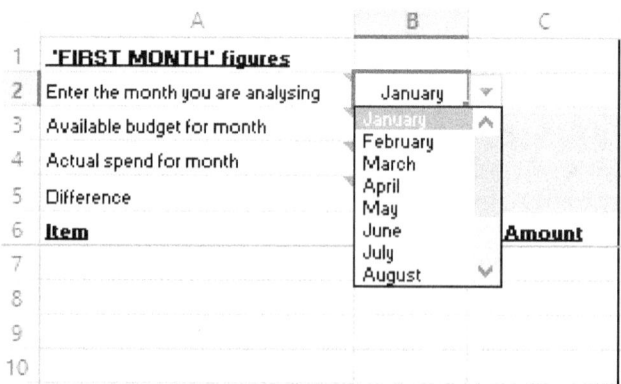

Select the month you want from the drop down menu that appears when you click on that cell in the 'FIRST MONTH' spreadsheet as shown above.

Notice, that as you select it, the system automatically loads the 'available budget' for that month into the cell below from the 'Master Account Planner (MAP)' spreadsheet we completed earlier. Believe it or not, you've already entered enough information for the spreadsheets to now start helping you by avoiding having to enter data more than once. So, for example, Jim and Alison, who are starting the exercise in February and are therefore analysing their first month of January, will see the following numbers appear:

	A	B	C	D
1	'FIRST MONTH' figures			
2	Enter the month you are analysing	January		
3	Available budget for month	1303.71		
4	Actual spend for month	0		
5	Difference	1303.71		
6	Item	Date	Amount	Fami
7				
8				
9				
10				
11				

Now all Jim and Alison have to do is enter every transaction that isn't one of the fixed or semi fixed transactions (as they have already covered these) from the statements that they previously sorted in Chapter 3. You'll see the results of that later on in this chapter. You will need to do the same, but this may not be as straightforward as it at first seems, depending on what your existing set up consists of.

If you are running with a joint account and pay everything out of it, this is obviously going to be easier than if you are a couple who keep their finances separate. A significant percentage of couples have entirely separate banking facilities and a loose agreement about who pays for what in a family environment, whether with or without kids. It's not for me to condone or commend one system over the other, but I can categorically tell you from experience that couples who do run separate systems tend to argue over money more, keep certain purchases secret and rarely work – financially – as a team. That said, couples with a joint account are sometimes convinced that the other partner is spending more than their 'share' or not contributing enough in the first place. Put it this way, it's very difficult to create a friction free environment when there is a 'my money' versus 'your money' scenario and even basic decisions like who will pay for the shopping can be contentious.

You may feel this doesn't apply to you which is great, but you may equally immediately recognise the symptoms. If the latter, I can assure you if you can find a way to implement this system together, it will yield exponential rewards far beyond what you can see at the moment. It's also critically important that you understand you're not giving up your independence – we'll be coming back to that later – but we are fine tuning your interdependence and creating a solid understanding moving forward.

For now, we're going to put in a 'work around' if your finances are separate just to get the information we need, but in the chapters ahead we'll deal with the issue square on so we can make the systems you're implementing work as seamlessly and as painlessly as possible. This will also eliminate any areas of possible conflict.

This *can* be the hardest part of the actual analysis, and much can depend on your relationship, your approach to this whole exercise and even the mood you're in. I have seen perfectly balanced discussions spiral into vicious arguments with shouting, sulking, huffing and puffing. Worse, before I really got to grips with the finer details of this system as I built it, I was even guilty of some of it. This is not designed to put you off as it is an absolutely essential part of the process, but I do want to make it clear that this part of the journey could be confrontational if not handled correctly. Forewarned is forearmed and there are a few things that are important for both of you to know.

If you have bought this book, the chances are that one or both of you realise that something has to change. If that's the case, then something you're doing isn't right. And if *that's* the case, it could be one or both of you who is the primary cause of the problem. What happened before is irrelevant, what only matters now is where you're going. Do not judge, condemn or question past purchases by the other partner, this is a transitional stage where we are eradicating past mistakes and agreeing to work together in the future. You will be far, far better off as a couple afterwards.

Be totally honest. You will need to list everything within the agreed timescale, most likely the last complete month. Do not hide or justify anything, just bite the bullet and list it.

By experience I can tell you that although this tends to be the most emotionally charged part of the process, the after effects are also the most emotionally rewarding. From this point on, there is no need for secrecy, deception or justification and the pressure release in some cases is incalculable. As a reminder again, you are NOT giving up your independence – everyone is entitled to their indulgences, purchases only for themselves and self-administered treats based on their own ideals and values - and you will both have that room for your own decisions going forward. Right now, we just need to know where the money goes each month.

The big red emergency button: If, despite everything I've said above, you still can't bring yourself to be 100% open, then, if you both agree, there is one other way that this will still (mostly) work. Simply list the expenses from your own accounts in categories grouped together, rather than individual items. So, for example, you might end up with a list like this:

Personal purchases	£245.80
Shopping for the family	£267.45
Social spending	£167.95 and so on ….

'Personal purchases' might include that snazzy pair of shoes you know you really shouldn't have bought and now feel slightly guilty about, or the latest tech gadget that seemed cool at the time and so on. 'Social spending' might include money spent down the pub or cash stuffed into a fruit machine. Try and come up with as many categories as you can because, by definition, the more you have, the more detail will be contained therein, but above all, make sure the numbers add up <u>exactly</u>. In other words, we need to account for every single penny that went through your accounts in the last full month.

Doing it this way will still yield key information, but be aware of the down sides. First, you must be confident in your maths as you add up the amounts in each case. Second, it gives you less information to work with when dong the analysis that follows. Finally, it *can* create a bit of friction in the home if not addressed. In almost every case, it's better to get it all out in the open as this gives you the best possible foundation going forward, not just from a financial point of view but (and probably more importantly) from a 'we're going to tackle this as a team' point of view.

Withdrawing cash from the bank account is worth a special mention. Clearly it's not always practical (or even possible) to break this down to the same degree of detail, so assumptions may need to be made. For example, it's fairly reasonable to assume that if you went out one evening and drew out £40 from the cashpoint, you will have spent it on that night out and it can be recorded as such. If you know, however, that you only spent £30 and then spent £10 on food at the local supermarket the next day, you could record it that way instead. The trick is to get it as accurate as possible whilst understanding that some degree of guesswork may be inevitable in those sorts of transactions.

That said, cash spend is much less common than it was even a few years ago. There is more and more focus on using cards directly, especially with the abolition of credit and debit surcharges making even very tiny transactions possible. These days, most people's interactions via card usually represent over 90% of their overall activity.

To complete the spreadsheet, all you need to do is enter each item as follows:

Description: A simple word is usually enough. You might write 'Supermarket' for family shopping or 'Coffees' if you grabbed a couple while you were out. I usually recommend writing the actual name of the supermarket or coffee house as this can help you even more when looking back. For example, if you find that you're spending more at a high end supermarket and you decide to cut down and move to a cheaper one, it's easy to see.

Date: Always use the same format dd/mm/yy. The spreadsheet is formatted for you, so if it doesn't look right, you may have typed it incorrectly.

Amount: Simply the amount in pounds and pence for each transaction. As explained before, always make sure that you use the exact amount to avoid errors later.

We'll also be using this part of the process as a final 'double check' that we have accounted for everything in the month by crossing off each transaction on the relevant statement(s) as you go. So, starting from the beginning of the month, add in the miscellaneous spend in the 'FIRST MONTH' as indicated above, and check each of the other transactions against your income and fixed outgoing sheets as well, just to make doubly sure it all looks right.

By the time you have finished, you should have crossed off every single transaction between the first and last date of the month you have chosen, whether income or outgoings. If that's the case for you when it's complete, you can move on to the final part of the book. If you find you have missed something, simply go back and assess where that transaction should sit and adjust the relevant section of the spreadsheet using the previous chapters as reference.

Armed with all this information Jim and Alison are now going to complete their first month. They've decided to work together and be totally open about the purchases they've made. They are also ignoring which account they're coming from since, going forward, they are going to change the way they manage their accounts and finances to the system recommended in this book anyway.

At the moment, both Jim and Alison have their own accounts where their respective pay goes into, and they both pay for things for themselves and the children on an ad-hoc basis, depending on who has money left when it's needed. They have a joint account they set up some time ago with a view of doing something a bit more formal with it, but they only 'half use' it, which means that some of the house bills come out from there and they transfer money in every now and again. They had some ideas about using it as a savings account as well for holidays and special treats, but in reality it simply never worked out that way as there never seemed to be enough money to do it.

In practical terms, this means both Jim and Alison will refer to their own statements and put their spend together on one sheet, almost certainly for the first time. They will also need to refer to their joint account in case anything was paid from there that they may not remember. In other words, they won't make any assumptions at all and will check every single transaction in the month to get the proper 'snapshot' that they need to make the rest of the book work properly for them.

After entering all the data from the January statements (which, as we saw at the beginning of this chapter is the month that they are working from) and confirming that all transactions in the month are accounted for, this is what their spreadsheet looks like now:

	'FIRST MONTH' figures		
1	**'FIRST MONTH' figures**		
2	Enter the month you are analysing	January	
3	Available budget for month	1303.71	
4	Actual spend for month	1632.74	
5	Difference	-329.03	OVERSPENT
6	**Item**	**Date**	**Amount**
7	Childcare	02/01/2018	59.70
8	Marks & Spencers	02/01/2018	10.50
9	Petrol	02/01/2018	36.45
10	Primark	02/01/2018	25.50
11	Sainsburys	02/01/2018	35.80
12	Costa Coffee	02/01/2018	5.50
13	Waitrose	02/01/2018	29.38
14	Gymnastics - Kids	04/01/2018	68.40
15	Sainsburys	04/01/2018	38.40
16	School dinners	04/01/2018	52.00
17	Tesco	05/01/2018	24.92
18	H&M	05/01/2018	63.18
19	Costa Coffee	06/01/2018	3.30
20	Petrol	06/01/2018	20.00
21	Childcare	06/01/2018	59.70
22	Hairdressers (Alison)	07/01/2018	25.00
23	Marks & Spencers	08/01/2018	14.76
24	itunes	10/01/2018	7.48
25	Topman	12/01/2018	85.00
26	Mail Order catalogue	12/01/2018	55.00
27	Sainsburys	12/01/2018	18.85
28	Petrol	13/01/2018	36.85
29	Birthday Meal Out - Prezzos	15/01/2018	76.80
30	Tesco	15/01/2018	97.18
31	Costa Coffee	15/01/2018	7.50
32	Haircut - Child 1	15/01/2018	9.00
33	McDonalds	15/01/2018	12.25
34	Jim's Birthday present from Alison	16/01/2018	69.99
35	Sainsburys	17/01/2008	35.70
36	Toolstation	17/01/2018	18.72
37	Tesco	20/01/2018	14.66
38	Homesense	20/01/2018	23.99
39	Petrol	21/01/2018	37.23
40	Royal Oak Pub	22/01/2018	15.65
41	Poundworld	23/01/2018	12.00
42	Sainsburys	23/01/2018	53.22
43	Childcare	25/01/2018	59.70
44	Dentists	25/01/2018	45.00
45	Decathlon	25/01/2018	48.20
46	Overdraft Interest	26/01/2018	3.62
47	Monthly bank charges	26/01/2018	15.00
48	Petrol	26/01/2018	35.84
49	Expert Phone - repair	29/01/2018	45.00
50	Morrisons	30/01/2018	76.80
51	Petrol	31/01/2018	44.02

55

The first thing that is obvious is the big bold 'OVERSPENT' warning that came on as they were entering their information, no doubt causing all sorts of alarm in the process. However, remember that this is the point of this exercise – we need to find out why Jim and Alison seem to be struggling and increasing the debt load over time despite a good income. It is clear that we now have the answer.

There is also a curious 'Actual Overspend Figure – Do not use until Chapter 10' which I am going to ask you to ignore completely at the moment as there's a few steps we need to complete before that number becomes useful.

At this rate, our couple will be needing to plug the gap to the tune of £3,948.36 a year (i.e. £329.03 x 12) and this will most likely manifest itself by a slowly increasing overdraft or credit card balance and a gradual awareness that money seems to be getting tighter. Over time, as charges mount, the rate of acceleration increases and Jim and Alison could, eventually, find themselves being another statistic in the world of debt collection, or, worse, insolvency. It may sound extreme and scary, but remember money itself is a completely unemotional, logical, mathematical entity. You have a finite amount and if the numbers don't add up, it leads to consequences and that's all there is to it. As simple as it sounds, there is very little preparation in life for money management and this is why so many people struggle at some point or another. Fortunately, Jim and Alison have spotted something isn't right and, whilst they have accrued debt as a result, they are not – yet – in serious trouble. Now they need to do a little more analysis and work out a solution.

You may find this reflects your own position. You may find you have a situation where your fixed out goings AND your monthly spend are BOTH showing a negative figure. If this is the case, I reiterate my earlier statement – do not panic and do not be tempted to abandon this process. Every step we take from this point is a step closer to solving the problem.

One thing that almost always comes up when I am doing this part of the exercise with people is the concept of 'one off' payments. I don't think I have ever done one of these where one or both of the partners have said something along the lines of "But this month was different because of x or y." We can see this in Jim and Alison's first month analysis as there are a few items that could easily fall into this category, the most notable ones being:

"Jim's birthday meal" at £76.80 on the 15th January

"Jim's birthday present from Alison" at £69.99 on the 16th January

"Dentist" at £45.00 for Jim who had an emergency filling done on 25th January

"Expert Phone – Repair" at £45.00 to replace the screen on one of the kids' phones.

That would be a total of £236.79 that was unplanned and would count some way towards the £329.03 overspend, right? It doesn't change that there is an overspend, but surely this gives us a reason (or perhaps 'excuse' is a more accurate word) as to why it exists. Technically this is correct, but this doesn't take into account life's little habits of catching you out when you're not looking. Let me expand on this a little.

Jim's birthday meal and presents are not really unplanned or 'one off' expenses. This is partly because they always know when it is and if there are four people in their family then they also know when *their* birthdays are and that in those months expenses may also be higher. If everyone has a birthday in a different month then they can say that those four months will have 'higher than usual' expenses. Except that they wouldn't be, because it would be the same every year.

In addition, Jim had to go to the dentist for an emergency filling and Alison took one of the kids' phones to the shop to get a new screen after the oldest one dropped it on the floor. This, arguably, is also not a monthly recurring payment (at least we'd hope not) so should they be 'penalised' for it, i.e. by going over budget? Well, let's put it this way - where else is the money going to come from?

Let's go further to make the point. There were no unusual car expenses in that month for Jim and Alison. No MOTs, no oil, replacement tyres or dings to fix, but there *could* be next month and, at the same time, Jim might not have to go to the dentist. What about February when the first payment for the kids summer camp is due, does that count as 'one off' (probably) and 'unexpected' (not really)? Alison has a night away booked in March with her girlfriends, where does THAT sit in the expenses? It's still the same, finite pot after all.

The point is that as you start to track these 'one off' expenses every month, you'll be amazed at how creative life gets to find ways to part you from your cash. There will be, literally every single month, something which you could class as 'unplanned' or 'one off'. The trick is to plan in advance for them and we'll be doing this in two parts, the first of which we can do right now. It's a simple statement which just helps focus your thinking and here it is:

Everything is a 'one off' monthly expense

That haircut? One off expense. Coffee? One off. Car repair? One off. The bottom line is, that unless it is a set direct debit or standing order, everything else you use your money for is a one off expense in some way. Of course it's a simplification, but it is based on a solid premise and experience of working with many people on this system. The fact is that most of us get hung up on what the definitions are and this can affect your clarity of thinking on it. So many times I have heard the "But that's only in THIS month" argument for it to be repeated over and over again before the penny drops. I even did it myself for the longest time before I understood it was never going to change, it was only what the money was being used *for* that was actually changing. There is always, ALWAYS something and once you can accept that, we can deal with the budgets in a much more controlled way.

The second part of this is having a budget set aside for emergencies, serious problems and, at the other end of the scale, holidays and treats, but we'll deal with all of this in due course and make it a standard part of our set up. You'll be amazed how quickly you can insulate yourself against all kinds of stress just by changing a few things that you'll barely even notice. However, we're not there yet. We need to deal with this overspend problem first and create a system going forward that gives both partners independence as well as making sure the family unit is covered.

Before we move on to the next stage I should mention credit cards. For many people, credit cards tend to be used for bigger, truly unexpected expenses (such as a big car repair bill) or holidays and then paid off over a convenient period and, on the whole, this has been the case for Jim and Alison. However, credit cards are increasingly being used for day to day expenses and Jim and Alison have found that they did a couple of transactions on them in January. One was for food shopping and one was for Alison's trip to the hairdressers that were put on credit when the account was temporarily dry. They have added these in to the first month analysis since they are actual, real expenses and the fact they came from a credit card account is not relevant when working out the monthly spend. In other words, these payments are being treated in the exact same way that payments from joint accounts or personal accounts are. In the end, it only matters that they are all counted, not where they came from.

This is a real alarm bell, however. If you are using credit for any day to day purchases, something is very wrong and needs to be fixed quickly. Jim and Alison have recognised that they are at the start of the 'slippery slope' in that interest and costs are going up with the total balance and they are going backwards. Eventually, they will reach the limits available to them and start looking for new ways to raise money via new cards or additional borrowing as many people do.

This gives the impression that the problem is solved, often leading to increased spending in the short term and a bigger problem in the long term. If you're already there, then you'll recognise this cycle, but even if you are, I reiterate again NOT to panic and to make sure you stay the course and complete this process wherever you may feel you are on that 'slippery slope.'

Many people now have a permanent balance on credit cards, so the interest is just a monthly expense that they get used to. We'll be dealing with how we make that go away as well in due course, but right now we need to assess how we structure our accounts going forward and to do *that*, we need to know how to break down the monthly payments and income in a simple and agreed way. This is the point at which both partners get clarity and independence and we'll be dealing with that in the next chapter.

Chapter Eight
Day to day spend: Yours, mine or ours?

We'll be coming back to the overspend issue a little later on, but to start with we need to work out who's spend is who's. This bit of analysis is the first step to setting up a system whereby all house and family bills are taken care of, but both partners have their own money to spend from their own accounts. There's many ways this can be done, but over the years I've found the easiest (and least problematic) way is to agree before we do the exercise what constitutes a 'house' or 'family' expense and set that in stone going forward. We'll use what is agreed here once and for all going forward so investing the time now saves a lot of hassle later on.

Using Jim and Alison's summary for the first month we can go through and find the ones that are usually the easiest to agree first of all. We'll be going through and putting each cost in one of three categories as we go – either 'Family', 'Jim' or 'Alison' and effectively we're trying to find a balance between all three ultimately. For now, however, we just need to put it in the right place.

Anything to do with the children is almost always a family cost, so all of these costs we will be able to place in the 'Family' column. We can do this simply by typing in the total amount for that entry in the corresponding column on the right hand side. As you can see from the example below, Jim and Alison have added in four numbers so far in the 'Family' column: Two childcare figures, one gymnastics figure and one school dinner amount. On each occasion, the spreadsheet checks that they have entered the number correctly and either 'OK' or 'ERROR' will appear on the greyed out column on the right. As you can see (overleaf), Jim has accidenty typed "58.70" instead of "59.70" on the bottom entry and the spreadsheet has let him know this is wrong. He simply enters the correct figure over the top and the error is solved. It is put there as a double check to ensure everything is accounted for correctly.

Item	Date	Amount	Family	Jim	Alison	Notes	CHECKER
Available budget for month	1383.71						
Actual spend for month	1632.74		TOTAL:	TOTAL:	TOTAL:		
Difference	-271.03	ENVELOPMENT	59.70	0.00	0.00		
Item	Date	Amount	Family	Jim	Alison	Notes	CHECKER
Childcare	02/07/2018	59.70	59.7				OK
Marks & Spencers	02/07/2018	11.50					
Petrol	02/07/2018	35.45					
Pret a	02/07/2018	25.50					
Sainsburys	02/07/2018	35.00					
Costa Coffee	02/07/2018	5.90					
Waitrose	02/07/2018	29.38					
Gymnastics Kids	04/07/2018	68.40	68.4				OK
Sainsburys	04/07/2018	37.40					
School dinners	04/07/2018	52.00		52			OK
Tesco	05/07/2018	24.02					
H&M	05/07/2018	63.18					
Costa Coffee	06/07/2018	3.30					
Petrol	06/07/2018	20.00					
Childcare	09/07/2018	59.70	58.7				ERROR

Food shopping is also always a 'Family' spend item, but there does need to be some clarity of understanding and a little give and take here. I have seen heated discussions about tiny items such as men's razors vs women's sanitary products and this goes against the spirit of the whole exercise. It's worth dealing with head on at this point because once the terms are agreed, it's easy to stick to.

My usual solution is to say that anything that is considered 'essential' for the couple, family home or individuals therein should be included in the normal weekly shop as standard and without issue. This would include the items mentioned above, as well as laundry items, cleaning items, and all the other essentials that we all need. Using that definition, it wouldn't *necessarily* include luxuries such as that high end anti-ageing cream or Jim's favourite designer after shave, or bottles of wine, CD purchases and so on. However, I would add this comment into the mix: In my experience, as long as both individuals in the relationship are reasonable and sensible, it's much easier just to say that all items *usually* included in the weekly shop will remain part of the 'family' spend going forward. At the end of the day, it usually evens out to such an extent that any difference is marginal anyway.

For example, Jim may drink more wine, but Alison likes premium quality fruit juices every morning and so on. In the end, we all have our own preferences and they usually balance with the other person's to some degree. Only if you think there is a serious imbalance in spend here (and remember we're only dealing with the typical weekly shopping items at this point) and that imbalance actually causes a problem do we need to work on it any further. If so, it'll require a further conversation about what should and shouldn't be included. Try and keep it very simple and be sensible about it – the simpler it is, the easier it is to run with going forward. At the end of the day, remember you are a couple, a single unit, and having that give and take works in all aspects of the relationship, not just when dealing with money. In Jim and Alison's case we do have a serious overspend issue that we need to come back to, but treat that as a separate issue for now and focus only on agreeing where the spend should sit. We'll be using the breakdown we saw earlier on page 55.

With our couple, it's Alison who does most of the shopping and she has a habit that can cause a bit of confusion with our tracking system. Instead of going to the cashpoint, Alison usually gets cashback at the till, which appears to add to the weekly shop and doesn't make it easily trackable as to where it's going. Both Alison and Jim have agreed going forward that what little actual cash they *do* spend, they'll get from the cashpoint so they can track it more easily, at least for the time being while they're dealing with the issue. It's not a big deal in their case as they don't spend much physical 'cash', but simple changes such as that can ultimately lead to a better understanding of where their hard earned money ends up.

If we assume, for the moment, that both individuals in the couple agree to include all items in the weekly shop as 'family spend', there is one more double check we need to complete. It might seem since we have entries from Waitrose, Tesco, Morrisons and Sainsbury's that we can just add all of these items immediately and, although 99% of the time that's correct, we might need to check what those spends consisted of. For example, Alison remembers that one of the supermarket visits, on the 20th January, was actually to the Tesco superstore where she bought a CD and book for herself while she was in town. This is perfectly fine, but it shouldn't be counted as 'family' spend and instead Alison puts it under her column. The same goes for the Marks and Spencer visit on the 2nd January where Jim met a friend for coffee in the café, and, as such should be included in HIS column.

Of course, this may all seem quite petty at this point, but you only need to do this analysis once and doing it properly will make it all so easy going forward. Essentially I am asking you to 'humour me' and follow the rest of the process. It will all make sense at the end of it.

The next item on the list is petrol, something that most couples usually underestimate as it's such an unavoidable cost and we tend to fill up on auto pilot as a result. I always strongly suggest that this remains a family spend item even if one person spends much more on it that the other since neither of you could go to work, ferry the children around or visit family without it. If you're in agreement, then all of these could be added to the family column as Jim and Alison have done. I would also usually include car repairs, oils, tyres, MOT's, services etc. no matter whose vehicle it technically is. Of course, those of you who are lucky enough to have a 'hobby' car such as a classic or specialist vehicle may choose to have any costs associated with THAT vehicle come from the account of the owner rather than the family account, but, as with all these things, it comes down to common sense.

Coffees appear three times in the month, once by Jim on his own, once by Alison with her friend and once when Alison bought some hot chocolates for the kids on a shopping trip. One is put in Jim's column, one in Alison's and one in the family column as a result.

The 'H&M' entry is mainly for kid's clothes, but Alison remembers that she also bought herself a very nice top for £20 while she was there. In this case, they split the entry £43.18 in the family column and £20 in Alison's column. It may not always be possible to remember these things on the first month analysis, but the more you can do, the better it will be.

The 'hairdressers' entry was for Alison as she wanted to get her hair coloured, so it goes under her column.

The 'iTunes' entry was for Jim as he's always downloading new apps on his phone. He adds it to his column.

'Topman' was also Jim's as he bought himself a new jacket in the winter sales.

Alison, meanwhile, had bought shoes from the 'Mail Order Catalogue' and enters the figure under her column.

I always suggest that any eating out as a family OR as a couple should be paid through the family account, including birthday meals. If, however, Jim or Alison were to meet friends without the rest of the family or their 'other half' I would recommend that this did not come through the family account in that circumstance. So, if Jim had met his friend for lunch one day, he would not pay for that through the family account, but his own.

'Jim's birthday present from Alison' is clearly a gift and gifts, traditionally, are purchased by the person giving it. Therefore this should come from Alison's account, just as presents the other way round would come from Jim's account. However, gifts for the children would usually come from the family account.

Jim needed to replace a lock on the front door and fitted it himself after buying it from Toolstation. This is clearly something that benefits the family as a whole and should come from the family account.

Alison spent the money at HomeSense on a new cushion and throw set for the sofa in the front room. The money comes from the family account.

Jim went to the pub with his friends for a round or two while Alison stayed at home with the kids, so the money spent should fall under his column.

The Poundworld expenditure of £12.00 was for some craft material for the kids who were making items for a school project. It is a family expenditure.

The dentist's expenditure is perhaps a trickier one and is the sort of thing that causes debate. Jim damaged his tooth and had to have an emergency filling – should this be a family expenditure or a personal one? There's no right or wrong answer of course, it all comes down to what you agree, but my usual suggestion is to break it down between essentials and luxuries. It's hard to argue that an emergency filling is not an essential item and my inclination would be to put it in under the family expenses. However, perhaps not all dental expenses fall under that category. Let's say, for example, one of our couple wanted to have a tooth straightened or cleaned up for cosmetic reasons, in other words, an entirely unnecessary procedure health wise, but something nice to do. I'd suggest putting that sort of work under each person's expenses for reasons that will become clearer later.

The Decathlon expense was for Alison who bought a new gym outfit for the New Year and so goes under her expenses.

The monthly bank charges and overdraft interest is classed as family expenses at this stage, but we'll come back to that later. It was low this month as our couple managed to keep a positive balance for longer in December by paying for most of Christmas on credit cards. However, they are yet to get the bill for this where the interest rate is likely to be considerably higher.

Finally, the only other entry that hasn't been allocated is the phone repair where one of the kids managed to break their screen and it needed fixing. This was done at a local shop and this expense, I would argue, is a family one as anything to do with the children usually is.

As Jim and Alison enter their final figures, the words "ALL ITEMS ASSIGNED" come up at the top of the screen in blue to let them know it's finished. This is an extra double check to show that the work has been done correctly. If you have not seen this yet, it means you still have some data to enter or assign somewhere, or there is a figure that isn't correctly set.

With Jim and Alison's example, I have tried to pick typical things that a typical family buys on a monthly basis using my own experience and that of helping other people, but the reality is that it could be very similar or completely different from your own situation. It doesn't really matter and you shouldn't get too stressed about it, the idea is to give you as many examples as possible so you can use those to work out the most likely place for each of your own expenses. Discuss it, agree it and put it in place, but remember nothing is set in stone and if you feel you need to revisit it in a month or two, then by all means do so. It's not unusual to take a couple of iterations to get it right.

The one thing that is almost universal when completing this exercise is just how small the individual partner's expenditure usually is when it comes down to it. As a family unit, or even just a well-established couple, the fact is that the vast majority of what you spend is spent together or as part of the family. This, of course, is in complete contrast to how we are as single people or when we're first getting together and tend to keep things separate. But this exercise has shown that we all still have a need to make our own money management decisions and that independence is important. It might be, for example, that Alison wasn't happy that Jim had spent £85 on a nice jacket just because it was in a sale, or that Alison had bought herself 'yet another' (in his view!) pair of shoes via mail order. That might be true in the context of the bigger picture where our couple are quite clearly overspending (and we'll come back to that point), but surely each partner should be able to buy what they want without the other silently resenting it as long as the family commitments are all taken care of?

For me, this is the secret, albeit rather obvious in retrospect, of making the whole system work. Jim and Alison MUST make sure that their family is secure, the bills are paid and that they are at least standing still, if not moving forward as their top priority. Anything beyond that, however, is 'luxury' spending and each partner should be able to decide where they want to spend it – and that is exactly what we will look at in the next chapter.

Chapter Nine
Setting up your bank accounts

There are two elements to this part of the process: First, we need to set up the physical accounts to match the process we'll be running and second we need to decide what amounts should go where in terms of those accounts.

The first part is straightforward and can usually be done very quickly with your existing banking provider. My recommendation here is almost always the same, that is, have one 'joint' account that you both have debit cards for (even a cheque book, if you use them, which can be signed by either party without needing to be countersigned) and a separate 'personal' account each. It is far, far easier to have them all with the same bank as you can do easy real time transfers if you need to and you'll each only need one log in to your phone app or online banking via a PC.

Each one of you would then see two accounts when logging in – one for your 'own money' and one for the 'family's money', which is effectively the joint account as we'll refer to it from now on. You'd also have two debit cards each in the same format. The reality is that you'd use the joint account for most items and only use your own individual account for those luxuries for yourselves or gifts for others.

The idea is that on the first day of each month, an agreed amount will be transferred from the joint account to each partner's personal account. At this point don't get hung up on detail about if your pay comes in on different dates etc., it's much easier to deal with monthly amounts on a calendar basis because our brains can naturally and easily understand that. The beauty of this system (once it is up and running properly) means that it really doesn't matter at which stage of the month the money comes in, it will always still work out correctly. The question is, however, what should that amount be?

Of course, our natural position is that we'd all like our own accounts to have the lion's share and we may even be able to justify it using a number of different arguments, the most common of which are "I earn more", "I work harder", "I have more hobbies", "I do much more with the kids" and a whole host of other variations that I have heard over the years. However, this is the old way of thinking and we're now working a single unit so we can put that to one side. And, of course, no two people in a couple are ever going to earn the exact same amount of money anyway!

This is part of the reason for doing the 'First Month' analysis. It may be a typical month (there's no such thing in reality as we've already seen) or it may not, but the fact is that it gives us a starting point for the discussion. For example, Jim realised that he was so busy with work in this month, he hardly went out at all in January and felt that he spent less than he normally would. Conversely, Alison bought new shoes, tops, a new gym outfit and bought Jim's present which she believes adds up to slightly more than she would normally spend. Once you have the actual numbers for a sample month it's much easier to get a feel for what they should be, after all, most of us, whether tracking our spend or not, are usually pretty good at knowing if we've overdone it.

In the end, after a short discussion, they decide to set their monthly personal budgets at £200 each a month. At first glance, this seems a tiny amount, just a miserly £2400 a year to spend on yourself and any Christmas/birthday presents you might be buying for your partner. It really doesn't seem that much until you consider that this is actually luxury money. There are no expenses to come out of here – no petrol, no mobile phones, no essential purchases etc. – just Jim or Alison money *for* Jim or Alison. This is money that either of them can spend at any time for themselves and they can manage it however they like. For example, Jim might decide to have another quiet month so he can buy something bigger the month after, whereas Alison might spend all her money now because she knows that in the school holidays she has less time for herself anyway and the cash will probably build up a little. Again, these are all example scenarios, you will need to tailor yours to your situation and how your home life works.

However, the total of the personal account budgets should never be more than around 30% of the total monthly available spend in my view. In Jim and Alison's case, without even realising it, they have set theirs at 30.68% (their £400 between them divided by the total available for the month which is £1,303.71) which is perfectly acceptable. They also have peace of mind, because they know that if they can manage the spending in the main account, they will be automatically managing all their bill payments, clearing debt AND saving up without having to actively manage or worry about it, as we shall soon see.

Now that Jim and Alison have decided this, they will need to go back to and update their main spreadsheet, the 'Master Account Planner (MAP)' and add in what they've decided. Remember, whilst this seems complicated and time consuming, we're still analysing and setting everything up for the future. Once all this work is done, it won't need entering again. They enter their agreed numbers on the sheet and it is copied across automatically as follows:

NOTE: A larger, clearer version of this image is available at www.originalcryptoguy.com under 'Books by Jason'

70

Our 'Master Account Planner (MAP)' spreadsheet is now almost complete and this final entry has now reduced the 'Disposable income total' figure by £400 since this figure is now the sum of what goes to each partner.

If you click back to it, you'll notice that this change also automatically adjusts the figure on the 'FIRST MONTH' analysis as we've now told it that the total available income is less than it was. This is not really a problem as that spreadsheet has now, mostly, served its purpose. Let's not forget also that £360.28 of it (The £121.93 that Jim spent in January plus Alison's £283.35) should now *not* be included here as we've passed that over, on paper anyway, to their individual accounts. We only now need to use the First Month spreadsheet to look at the thorny issue of overspend, which is a serious issue for our couple. But first, we need to finish off our account set up and there's one final step to do.

Whilst we have looked at our monthly spend, we now need to quickly re-examine and double check the direct debits and other fixed costs. Remember, these are normally things that are to do with the house or family and cover all the essentials, but we do need to do a double check – should any of these transactions come from the individual partner accounts instead of the main joint account?

The 'usual suspects' that lead to discussion are the ones that have someone's name on them, in this case life insurance, mobile phone bills and gym membership. My personal view is that life insurances should always be paid by the joint account as they affect everyone, so that one is relatively straightforward, but what about mobile and gym payments?

There are many schools of thought here and it depends on your circumstances and what you agree to be the best way forward. It could be that all mobile bills should be included in the joint account as standard or that they should be separated out into each individual's account but with a slight, perhaps disproportionate increase in their monthly payments. For example, both Jim and Alison's mobile bills are quite high at the moment, but because these are being paid by the joint account, there's perhaps not as much incentive to reduce them as there would be if they were paying them directly. So, Jim and Alison might agree to put their own bills in their accounts, but increase their monthly allowance by slightly less than the full amount of the usual bill, say £50 each. In other words, their own monthly account income would now increase to £250 a month instead of £200, but they'd have to each bear the cost of their own mobile phones. By doing this, the joint account is already £22.50 a month better off, and both of them have an incentive to find better deals so that they will have the money to spend themselves.

These are only two possibilities, and Jim and Alison are showing that they are already thinking ahead. They know for sure now that they are over spending, so they also know they have to cut costs going forward and this may be the first step. They could, for example, combine plans which might give them a better deal and this could then just stay in the joint account. They could also agree to swap to free or low cost apps such as WhatsApp or Snapchat rather than paying for text or images etc.

As is so often the case when dealing with accounts, money and people, having a good understanding of the overall picture is very helpful when making these decisions. Whichever way you go, remember to check your spreadsheets are correct; if you move the mobile bills to your accounts, remember to adjust your monthly income upwards (if that's what you're doing) and delete them from the joint account, or leave them as they are if you agree to carry on as before.

Alison's gym membership is also fairly straightforward, but for different reasons. This is most likely a luxury item and should be a deduction from Alison's account rather than the joint account and done without a corresponding increase in her monthly payment. Whilst decisions like this seem harsh at first, they do make sense. After all, only Alison benefits from it, it's effectively a hobby she enjoys and she can control the cost, i.e. whether she spends it or not. It's no different to Jim going out to play golf one afternoon with a friend and spending £45 on turf fees – this should NOT come from the joint account, just Jim's.

Again, in the context of cost savings, Alison may well be incentivised to reduce her membership fees perhaps by changing gym or moving to a cheaper tariff. She goes online and finds she can have the same membership at the same gym for £25.99 instead of £45.99 as long as she switches to the day time plan meaning she can't go in the peak times before 10am in the morning. Since Alison has never been at that time, preferring to go on her days off from her part time job, this is a perfect solution and she moves the now reduced direct debit to her own account. The joint account can now be amended yet again by deleting the gym membership entry on the 'Master Account Planner (MAP)', thus making an extra £45.99 available to spend on family related items.

This is also a good example of why it is so important to revisit fixed costs from time to time. The fact is that things change all the time and companies are not known for helping their customers pay lower amounts. With the gym, for instance, they will almost certainly have known that Alison would benefit from a lower payment due to her entry and exit times, but they have no incentive to tell her that. It will be the same for every company that you deal with, so regular checks and asking for the best deal is always worthwhile. I have – genuinely – seen situations where families have saved hundreds of pounds *a month* by revisiting payments, benefits and contracts that were set up years ago and were no longer relevant to them.

To delete the figure from the spreadsheet, simply highlight the whole row and select 'delete.' Doing this will adjust the 'FIRST MONTH' spreadsheet, but it won't matter as it has done its job.

Jim and Alison, and by extension YOU, have now completed most of the set up. We know what our debits are, we know where any problems lie and we also know what spend should be coming from where. We can now to move on to dealing with the problems we've identified and managing the monthly payments in such a way that we'll never end up back at this point. Give yourself a little reward, you deserve it for all your work and effort so far. However, the best is yet to come. We're about to tell money stress where to go once and for all.

<u>Chapter Ten</u>
Taking control of spend and debt

Up until now we've been backwards looking. That is, we've looked at what we've already spent and used it to create a basis to go forward. However, the reality is that doing the exercise itself almost always changes where we're going in the future. We can now see, probably for the first time, what needs to be done.

There are two parts to this next section: we need to know how to fix our overspend and how to set ourselves up for the future to avoid any nasty surprises. It would also be nice to actually get some pleasure from the money we work so hard to make in the first place. We'll need to deal with it in that order, because the second part won't work until the first part is resolved.

I will give you some tools and techniques to help address overspend, but much of the success here will come from you. You will need to be honest about what each item is and utterly brutal with expenses if you're in a similar situation to Jim and Alison. At the end of the day, the amount going out MUST be less than or equal to the amount coming in, or you'll just be slipping further and further backwards. There is no other way to do it – we must make the numbers work.

When I sit and take couples through the entire process in this book, I usually do it in three sittings and ask for some preparation to be done for each. I request that all paperwork is put together and sorted before I get there for the first sitting where we will usually complete everything up to this point using the same spreadsheets I am providing you with as a result of buying this book. This usually takes a few hours and I then set the homework of looking at the inevitable overspend which includes both the fixed outgoings (that we've already touched on) and the items that have been spent from the joint account. When I come back, usually a day to two later, we'll then go through each line and assess whether we can make it smaller or not. We'll almost always complete everything else in this book at that second meeting. However, I'll usually do a third visit a few weeks later to double check everything is in place and is working for the family concerned, making any little tweaks where necessary.

This part, that of going through and really analysing the money that has been spent in detail, can sometimes take the lion's share of that meeting. We get really aggressive about what can be saved, trying to achieve an underspend if possible. The first month after installing the system is usually the most painful, but it is also the most rewarding, knowing that you're in control and things will now get better over time rather than worse. It's a bit like pushing a car – it's hard at first but as you get the momentum going it gets easier and easier. If you give up before you're really rolling, you run the risk of coming to a stop and then trying to start again, only this time with less energy and belief you can do it. Yes, you'll almost certainly have a tough month or two or even more ahead, but I can absolutely assure you it will lead you to a better place than you were heading. So let's take the bull by the horns and get it done.

We'll be using the 'FIRST MONTH' spreadsheet again to start with, even though we've now played with the income figures a bit by adjusting the numbers on the 'Master Account Planner (MAP)' spreadsheet. That's OK because we're really only interested in a couple of the actual numbers, the rest is about how we're spending it. On Jim and Alison's spreadsheet, their available spend for the month is now shown as £949.70 which is what we're saying it *should* have been if we'd added in their personal monthly allowances at the start of the month. This seems to imply an overspend of £683.04 but this is misleading since this still includes their own spend items, so we need to take that out again.

So, an 'overspend' of £683.04 MINUS the things that Alison spent in her column and MINUS the things that Jim spent in his column gives a **real** overspend figure of £322.76. By no coincidence, this is the mysterious figure shown in the 'Actual Overspend – Use for Chapter 10 only' box at the top of the spreadsheet that I'd asked you to ignore previously. Now is the time we're going to use it.

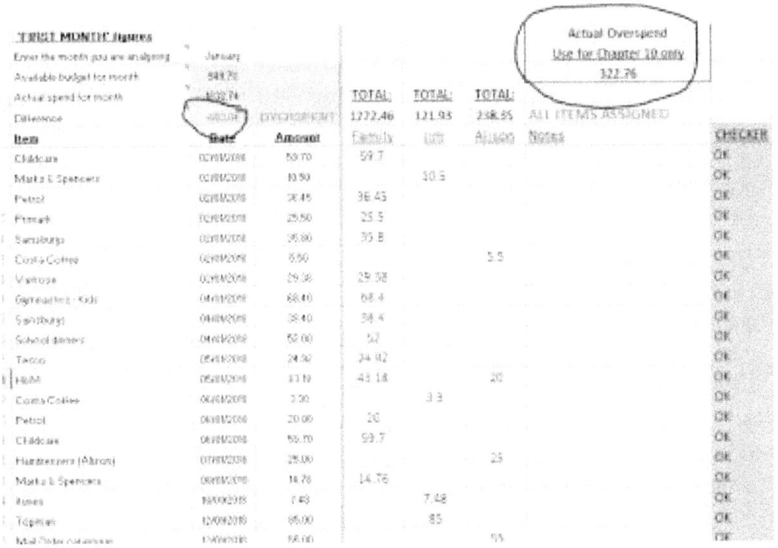
January
TOTAL:
TOTAL:
TOTAL:
1272.46
121.93
ALL ITEMS ASSIGNED
Item
Amount
Notes
CHECKER
Actual Overspend
Use for Chapter 10 only
322.76

NOTE: A larger, clearer version of this image is available at www.originalcryptoguy.com under 'Books by Jason'

This is our magic number, the one that we have to satisfy to make our monthly spend work properly going forward and it's a big one in real and percentage terms. In reality, as we'll see later, the number is even bigger, but right now, because we're dealing with historical spend and we can't change it, this will be fine to work with.

Whilst doing this exercise, remember that the data only tells us so much, there's the real world to consider as well and this will become clearer as we go through some examples. There may also be some quick wins we can find and implement easily, but everyone's situation will be different. Let's go through the list and see what we can work out.

Childcare is a big expense for our couple in relative terms as it is for most working parents with young, dependent children. Is there another way to manage this? Are there after school clubs that the kids could attend that might be cheaper? Or school activities? Are there crèches at work? Or family that could help out once or twice or week? It's possible, of course, that there's nothing that can be done here, but focussing on it and revisiting the set up quite often yields different solutions that hadn't been considered before. Childcare is one of those costs that tends to come about because of routine and once that routine exists we don't tend to question it again. Perhaps it is time to do so.

Jim and Alison spend £52 a month on school dinners because it is more convenient than packed lunches. Is this worth changing? Would it be cheaper if they made the meals themselves?

In truth, I wouldn't consider Jim and Alison's monthly spend overly frivolous in any way, apart from a few items that have now been moved to their own accounts. But they ARE spending more than they can afford compared to what they're earning and what they have committed to in terms of fixed outgoings. This means they have no choice but to find ways to cut down, and quickly. It's worth remembering that whilst this transitional period may seem a little (or even a lot) painful, it's not forever. Right now, this is only about taking back control which has to be the top priority.

It's always worth looking at the overall shopping bill to see if something can be done here. They have spent £439.67 across several shops in the month which works out to be around £101.46 a week or £14.49 a day. This is really not too bad in my view, especially for a family of 4, but they did spend much less this month because they had spent so much in December and were still using up leftovers well into January - a good example of remembering that you're dealing with 'real world' issues. In reality, this means their bill is probably closer to £500 a month, and let's not forget that they are also paying for school dinners as well. Adding all this up, we're looking at closer to £127.40 a week.

What you think about spending this much on food shopping depends on many factors. I know families who could not imagine spending that much in a month on food and groceries. I know of others who will have spent Jim and Alison's entire monthly budget in a week - and more - on top of that. Food and grocery shopping seems to naturally reflect the amount of money we 'feel' we have more than any other spend, even if that feeling isn't quite correct. My personal view, however, is that there is always something to be done here. The reality is that most of us are 'lazy' shoppers, and will tend to pick up anything that catches our eye in supermarkets which, incidentally, these businesses rely on to make their profits. The way to beat this is to be prepared with a clear idea of what to get and then stick to it.

I also like to set couples I'm working with a challenge for the first month if they are suffering from extreme overspend – try and feed the family for X amount, just for that month, where X is normally a figure based on their own level of spend. It's set at a very hard level to achieve, but because my last visit is usually a month later, people generally make the effort to do it and surprise themselves, creating new habits at the same time. It's usually done by switching to lower cost supermarkets, planning carefully and (a big favourite and something we're all guilty of from time to time) using everything in the cupboards. For Jim and Alison, I'd set their spend level for the month at a tricky, but possible, £250 for the first month.

Of course, these days, there's all sort of websites and books to help, offering coupons, discounts, advice on where to find the cheapest of this or that, and literally hundreds of super healthy budget meal recipes. Some 'own brand' substitutes are even healthier than the originals and there are dozens of TV programmes and YouTube channels dedicated to the subject. In truth, we have more facilities available to us than ever before, but sometimes we need something to push us to find and use that information, such as a financial issue. Remember also this is not for ever – once we're sure we're in full control of our spend, there's no reason why the occasional treats and pre-prepared food items can't be added back in if the budget will accept it. Even better, as we get our debts under control and start to reduce the monthly outgoings, we will, over time, free up extra monthly funds to spend on the family or save for something nice, such as a holiday, even if we don't manage to secure an increase in our income.

In Jim and Alison's case, for example, we can see that their last payment on their car loan is in October, meaning that they will have an extra £195 a month available from November onwards.

For now however, it's worth questioning absolutely everything at this stage. It's also worth remembering that any savings we make, no matter how small, are now being tracked and make a real difference to our financial situation rather than being lost in the chaos that reigned before. In other words, if we get something for £5 less than we were paying before, we can now immediately, and in real terms, use that £5 somewhere else. So let's continue with our expenses for the month and see what else we can 'claim back'.

Petrol is always a big household expense so is there anything that can be done here? Is cycling or walking to work or school a possibility? What about car sharing or even small things such as planning shopping trips better so they are all done once or twice a month rather than several times as they are now? Here's a big one – do we actually NEED two cars? How many times have we heard a story about someone whose car went into the garage and it got stuck there for a week or so? Then, whilst it was there, they realised they hadn't even missed it? It happens all the time, and whilst it's not viable for everybody, it is one of those things that you'd never consider if you didn't have to.

Eating out and other luxuries may need to go on hold for the moment and little, non-critical expenses (such as the Homebase cushion and throw set) don't need to be made right now. I'd even argue that a cracked phone screen replacement isn't immediately necessary – it's possible to use simple screen covers as a temporary fix and most phones work indefinitely with a cracked screen anyway. Why not put it as a low priority expense and fit it in a month where there are funds available? After all, you'll be able to see from now on when that may be.

As with all of these discussions, the possibilities are endless both in terms of what you're spending and what you can do about it. Short term sacrifices almost certainly will need to be made, and at the end of the day it will be *you* who decides what changes – this book can only provide the framework in which to work. However, don't get too hung up on what you HAVE spent – that money has already gone – instead use this a basis to think about how you WILL spend going forward. And, of course, our daily spend is only part of it, we will need to look at the fixed expenses as well as there may well be things we can do there too.

On Jim and Alison's 'Master Account Planner (MAP)' spreadsheet, we can see that things like water rates and TV license are almost certainly set in stone, but there are things hidden in plain sight that we can address. Home insurance, for example, certainly isn't. Their premium isn't bad, but it's certainly not the best and it should be possible to shave around £8 a month off the cost, giving us an extra £96 a year for luxuries, debt repayment or day to day spend. The point is that we have *the choice*.

Looking at the debits as a whole, it strikes me immediately that there are two payments for TV packages and phone and internet packages since they are using two different companies totalling a not-insignificant £76.25 a month. Some quick research reveals that they can get an almost identical service on all three by combining it and saving another £23 a month, or £276 a year.

Jim and Alison took out separate mobile phone insurance years ago and have been paying it ever since, but as part of this exercise Jim has realised that they have full mobile insurance cover as part of their bank account package AND it's included in the home insurance policy. This means this is an entirely useless policy that can be cancelled immediately and it may be possible to save even more on the home insurance as well. In any case, that's another £8.50 a month, or £102 a year, that can be added to the savings pot. In just a short time, Jim and Alison have now saved £39.5 a month, or £474 a year without losing any benefit at all.

Further savings are likely, even if not immediately, by revisiting other insurances, tariffs for electricity and gas, and, as mentioned before, mobile phone bills. If Jim and Alison can cut these by another £30 a month, they'll end up with nearly £80 a month, or almost £1,000 a year, extra to spend on debt reduction, daily spend or luxuries. This is work that only needs to be done once – once it's done a new set of direct debits stay in place giving you the saving automatically each month, but, as we've already seen, regular reviews, especially on renewal, should be done routinely and thoroughly to avoid wasting your hard earned money.

With your own fixed costs, be ruthless and question everything. Think out of the box. Do you even need your landline? Can you get a better mortgage deal? Can you combine services, get better tariffs or switch to a cheaper supplier? I can honestly say that in all the years of helping people go through this process I have never seen a situation where *some* savings weren't possible in both the short and medium term, so this is an important part of the exercise.

Of course it takes a bit of time, usually a month or two, to get the full benefit of these changes, so I always suggest leaving the fixed costs as they are for the moment and working with the worst case scenario - you'll get a greater benefit later on because you'll have formed spend habits that suit lower disposable income levels. Because the spreadsheets are all linked, you can simply amend the costs as the savings come in and your spendable income will change automatically for the month. We'll learn how to make those changes later. In Jim and Alison's case, they'd set the figure for the mobile phone insurance to zero the month after they cancelled it and then adjust the other figures as savings are achieved, giving them more and available income each time.

You'll notice that I haven't mentioned credit cards again, and this is deliberate. Personally, I believe that credit cards can be very useful for very specific short term purposes, but if you do not clear your credit card in full each month and have a balance carrying forward each time, you are throwing away very significant sums of money that could be spent on your family instead. It also makes saving utterly pointless as the opportunity cost of using that money to reduce the monthly interest will always be more than the money you'll save. This is the moment when we commit to getting rid of them forever. I'd strongly suggest taking them out of your wallet or purse and putting them somewhere extremely inconvenient to discourage use. If you're really brave, destroy them by cutting them in pieces and throwing them away. If you're not there yet and are worried about how you'll pay the bills next month without them, that's ok too. For now, just make them the lowest priority form of payment until you are ready, but understand that continued use of these cards will condemn you to always throwing money away and never being able to get full control. In this context it's a bit like giving up a powerful and addictive drug; it's very hard to do, it's extremely scary and life seems impossible without it. Just ask a smoker who's decided to quit and is at the beginning of the process. This really is no different in many ways and just shows the level of change you now realise you need to make to get control of everything. Fortunately, we're doing it in a controlled and very well tested way that we know – categorically – will lead to positive results.

The beauty of installing and running this process – i.e. the spreadsheets and bank account set up – is that the credit cards will, eventually, be taken care of by default without you having to think about it. Most couples I have dealt with only ever make the minimum payment which varies as the amount changes over time. Credit card companies are big fans of these people because they make enormous profits out of them year after year through extremely high interest rates. If you're at that stage, like Jim and Alison are, further interest is going to be unavoidable but we'll be reducing it over time and eventually take back control in full so long as no more spend goes on to those cards – ever – until they are back to zero. It'll also do wonders for your credit rating, by the way, and the irony is that you may well find those same companies will keep giving you increases in your limits to entice you to spend more. Don't be fooled, they're not being nice guys, they can see their profits dropping and this a proven and justifiable way to boost them again. After all, they can show that you can manage the payments, right?

There is an action to take right now though. If you pay by sending a cheque, or making a manual online payment, we need to change that process to a standing order or a fixed direct debit if your company will allow it. You might need to contact them to set it up, but the objective is to set an amount that is fixed each month rather than paying the minimum amount each month. This is because the minimum amount is really engineered so that the credit card companies can maximise their profits as you pay down the debt, whereas setting a fixed amount will gradually increase the rate you clear it off and significantly reduce the interest.

What you set this for depends on your financial situation. It is far better to be consistent and affordable than it is for it to be a stretch which might cause extra spend from time to time on those cards. In Jim and Alison's case, they have a significant overspend to deal with and they are going to have a tough couple of months ahead as they adjust and get their cost savings set up. In that case, I would suggest paying only this month's minimum payment but then setting it as a fixed amount, which is what they've already done effectively in their 'Master Account Planner (MAP)' spreadsheet. On this spreadsheet, you can see that Credit Card A and Credit Card B already have a fixed, rather than reducing, amount next to them each month, and they will clear these much faster as a result. Also, because it IS the same payment each month, they will notice no difference in their overall spend each time. Their debts are being paid automatically.

Eventually, these balances will go to zero and the payments can stop. Jim and Alison currently pay £531.05 in debt repayments, so they'd be very happy having all that money spare each month at some point in the future. Their debt level (excluding mortgage) is about 16% of income which, although higher than we'd like, is certainly not as high as some I've seen which can run at well over 50% or more. But to almost any levels of debt, the same principles of what we're doing here apply. If your debts are *very* severe (and by this I mean most or all of your monthly income is going on debt repayment) you might want to look at Chapter 14 for some extra information on this and some resources that you might want to use. I still offer the same advice – don't panic or stress, all problems are ultimately solvable, all bad times ultimately pass and realise you can only learn from the past, not change it. The lessons and processes in this book will also ensure that it will never happen again. So if extra action over debt does need to be taken, you will still be able to apply everything you've learned so far, using the same spreadsheets and set up in the same way, to help you once you're in a position to move forward again.

I have to add a word of congratulations at this point - **you have now completed around 90% of the entire set up process!** You have successfully identified the problem areas, you have set a plan to reduce and eventually get rid of debt over time and you should now feel – to some degree or another - that it's you who are in control of where you're going financially. Our last piece of the puzzle is to look at how we keep track of everything and how we protect ourselves against those inevitable unexpected costs without resorting to credit cards or other debts. It really is possible and the next chapter will show you how.

Chapter Eleven
Protecting against bad things, saving for good things

It's pretty clear that Jim and Alison, despite earning a very good wage, were heading for trouble. Because of that wage, they may well have managed to borrow more and kept going as they were for months or even years hence, but eventually the numbers were never going to add up. They now understand that they will have a few tough months ahead and they will need to be very strict about their spend for a period of time, but they can now see – visually via the spreadsheets - that it will work out going forward.

They also know that their net worth (the amount they are actually worth when they add up everything they own and take off the debt) is likely increasing steadily, which means they are going forward every single month rather than working hard to go backwards. It's a very liberating thought and it means they are securing their future at the same time as a by-product of managing their day to day money decisions correctly.

But there's still a few more eventualities we need to cross off the list before we can say we have everything covered. How will we manage savings? How will we deal with emergency payments, such as an unexpected car repair bill? How do we plan for a holiday? Fortunately, all of this is built into the spreadsheet system too.

We've already covered that it is not worth saving if you have debt outstanding that has a higher percentage interest rate than anything you would achieve by putting it away. This will *always* be the case since institutions lend at a higher rate than they borrow, but it is prudent to have some easily accessible savings at all times. Some people argue that it is better to throw everything you can at credit cards to get the interest payments down and then simply use them if you need to. I don't necessarily disagree with this view and actually advocated it myself in the beginning, but over time I've found that this method is usually not as effective as not using the credit cards at all and putting a reserve in place a different way. Using the cards "just occasionally" requires a little more work in tracking but also seems to create a psychological state whereby it is OK and easily justifiable to use them in such a way that extra spend inevitably occurs and the problem isn't, in fact, solved. It seems to come down to self-discipline and focus which some people are better at managing than others. It would be my strongest possible suggestion based on years of experience, therefore, to follow THIS process instead, let the debts reduce naturally and put some security in place another way.

We've already done the hard work in terms of setting everything up, from now on this is about 'real world' use. For this, we're going to switch to another spreadsheet called 'Budget Manager' which you can select by clicking on the corresponding tab at the bottom of the screen, in the same way as you did previously. This is the place where you will probably spend more time than any other sheet on a day to day basis as it is where you will be tracking what you are spending and seeing what you have left for the month. However, for now, we just need to get started and understand how our 'savings' system will work.

This sheet has the twelve months of the year set up for you, but you will only need to start where it is relevant to you. In Jim and Alison's case, for example, since they did all their analysis for January, they will be starting their tracking in February and will need to put an 'x' in the cell under where it says 'Start this month? (x)' in that month, as shown below in the top circle on the next image:

MONTHLY BUDGET MANAGER						
Month	JANUARY	Start this	Month	FEBRUARY	Start this	Month
Start budget	0.00	month? (x)	Start budget	1093.70	month? (x)	Start budget
Prior month adjust	0.00		Prior month adjust	0.00	x	Prior month a
working total	0.00	saved	working total	1093.70	saved	working tot
10% savings	0.00	0.00	10% savings	984.33	109.37	10% saving
SPENT	0	0.00%	SPENT	0	0.00%	SPENT
LEFT TO SPEND	0.00	0.00%	LEFT TO SPEND	984.33	100.00%	LEFT TO SP
Item	Date	Amount	Item	Date	Amount	Item

This immediately populates the figures for February from the other sheets and ignores January since they used that as their first month just for analysis. In your case, don't worry if you're not actually starting on the first day of your chosen month, we can add anything that's missing to bring us up to date in due course as we'll see in the next chapter. For now, however, we're just concerned with the 'saved' figure that is also shown in the image in the bottom circle.

This figure is calculated automatically. It is 10% of your available spend after all fixed debits have been taken care of and its job is to put that money aside right at the start of the month before you have spent a single penny. This is deliberate, because if you treat your 'savings' or 'emergency fund' (whatever you want to call it) with the same discipline that you treat your fixed direct debits, you'll always have money available if you need it quickly and it will build up over time.

The money, however, doesn't physically go anywhere, it remains in the joint account and it is the first step to unlinking your bank account balance with what you have available to spend. This statement, although seemingly innocuous, is actually extremely important and, in many cases, is one of the main reasons I have seen so many people get into trouble. Let's face it, if you've just been paid and you see a big bank balance, you think "I can spend a load of money because I have a load of money". Of course, you have some vague idea that there are debits and commitments in there somewhere, but that's ages off and, well, there's SO much in there, right? This way of thinking is not uncommon at all and it's really, really easy to do, especially if you have no tracking system in place. If you recognise that way of thinking to any degree, or something similar, you may have found yourself in a classic 'more month than money' situation and this is the reason why it happens. We consider this 'normal' as we're so used to hearing other people say the same thing, because the fact is that most people fall into the same trap.

The reality is that from now on, you are not going to be governed - or even influenced - by your bank account balance in any way. The only thing that matters now is what your spreadsheet says and we'll be completing that whole process in the next chapter. At this point, we just need to understand that a higher bank balance than is showing on the spreadsheet does NOT mean that we have extra money to spend. It's there for a reason. It's being put aside.

This figure links to our final spreadsheet called 'Saving & Emergency' which you can access by clicking on the appropriate tab at the bottom of the screen as usual. Using Jim and Alison's example, their spreadsheet looks like this:

	A	B	C	D	E	F
1	**Saving and Emergency Funds**					
2	You are automatically saving each month!					
3						
4	January	0.00		SAVING AND EMERGENCY FUND TOTAL		109.37
5	February	109.37				
6	March	0.00		*Spending of saving and emergency fund:*		
7	April	0.00		Description	Date	Amount
8	May	0.00				
9	June	0.00				
10	July	0.00				
11	August	0.00				
12	September	0.00				
13	October	0.00				
14	November	0.00				
15	December	0.00				
16						
17						
18						
19						
20						
21						
22						
23						
24						
25						
26						
27						
28						
29				TOTAL OF SAVING/EMERGENCY FUND SPENT:		0
30						
31				Left in fund		109.37
32						

You can see that February's saving figure of £109.37 has been added in automatically and the grand total is shown on the right hand side. Since they're only working on this one month so far, that's all they'll see at the moment.

Hopefully, they won't use any of their fund in February and if so, it will be added to next month's savings figure and it'll build up quickly. At the same time, they are meeting all their bills, paying down their debts and controlling their spend simply as a function of using the spreadsheets and applying what they've learned. If they do have to use a little, they will simply enter it in the columns indicated and it will be deducted from the running total.

Of course, there may well need to be some discussion about what this fund can be used for, but most couples tend to agree this relatively easily as this really applies to unexpected essential expense such as car repairs or work that needs doing on the house, such as boiler repair work etc. However, most people extend this slightly to include a wider definition; that of turning this 'emergency' fund into something that could also be positive, such as savings for a very nice treat, a holiday, or a lump sum to clear debt faster. After all, if you have managed to have a good run and have saved a few hundred pounds, there is no reason why it couldn't be used for one of these more preferable options. The best way to do this is to set a date, perhaps six months in the future or simply at the end of the year, when you will have a look at what is left and agree how to spend it – perhaps at one of your 'board meetings!' I always suggest, however, leaving a certain amount, perhaps equivalent to one month, in the account so that if something does go wrong immediately after you've spent it, you're still covered. I'd also suggest that if you are constantly using your overdraft you use this 'extra' money to gradually pay it off. Not only are you giving yourself more control by not being beholden to a bank, it will save you money in interest and fees which you can spend on someone far more deserving – YOU!

By employing this system, you are effectively doing the opposite of what most people do, which is saving the money *before* spending it. Usually, we'll naturally reach for credit if there's something we want (or are being forced to pay) and pay for it later, but this is expensive and exposes us to risk if something (else) goes wrong. It is the single most common cause of runaway debt and we've all been conditioned to one degree or another that this is the 'normal' thing to do. It is, of course, but that doesn't mean it's the *right* thing to do and this has only really been a phenomenon of the last forty or so years. The good news is that by following this system you can still have many of the nice things in life, just perhaps a little later, but this time with total peace of mind. It's a great feeling!

Chapter Twelve
Spend and take stock

Going back to our 'Budget Manager' spreadsheet, we now need to get into the habit of understanding it and, most importantly, keeping it up to date. This is usually the responsibility of one partner, but both should be able to refer to it easily and quickly without drama, hesitation or confrontation.

Entering the data requires a little discipline in the form of a couple of minutes each day, but it really isn't that hard, especially when most people have easy access to PCs and laptops these days. But before we get to our daily updates, we need to make sure that we get any initial entries correct.

Since it's unlikely that we'll be starting on the first of the chosen month, we just need to add in anything we've spent so far in our first 'proper' month. So, in Jim and Alison's case, since they used January as their analysis period and are now in February, they will need to enter anything they have spent thus far using their bank statements in much the same way as they did for that first month analysis in January. For argument's sake, let's assume it's February 12th when they are finally ready to go. So, using their online or app based banking, they go through and add the items they've spent that should have come from the joint account into the spreadsheet.

When they have done that, it looks like this:

Month	FEBRUARY	Start this
Start budget	1093.70	month? (x)
Prior month adjust	0.00	x
working total	1093.70	saved
10% savings	984.33	109.37
SPENT	265.26	26.95%
LEFT TO SPEND	719.07	73.05%
Item	Date	Amount
Charity Donation	01/02/2018	6
Childcare	01/02/2018	59.5
Petrol	02/02/2018	46.52
Lidl	05/02/2018	17.87
sainsburys	06/02/2017	16.09
school lunches	07/02/2017	29
poundland	09/02/2018	11
itunes	10/02/2018	5.48
sainsburys	12/02/2018	32
sainsburys	12/02/2018	11.25
Petrol	12/02/2018	28.55

This shows us straight away that Jim and Alison have made a cracking start to the month and are really working on their spend levels. They have cut their school lunches cost for the month and are experimenting with packed lunches, although they have not yet found any solutions for childcare. The big grocery shop they did right at the end of January set them up well and only a couple of small top up shopping trips have been done so far, although it's clear another large one is due soon. Alison is also trying cheaper supermarkets to see if she can make savings without compromising on healthy meals, something she really believes in. The bottom line is, though, that they have only spent 26.95% of the budget so far and are nearly half way through the (albeit short) month. It's great work.

However, because this IS their first month, some of the expenses shouldn't be there. Neither Jim or Alison have claimed 'their' £200 this month as the direct debits haven't kicked in yet, although they are now in place ready for the next month, i.e. March. As a result,

Jim's iTunes payment of £5.48 and Alison's CDs that she bought at Sainsbury's for £11.25 have come from the joint account rather than their own accounts. This is easily solved by logging in to their online banking and manually transferring the money for this month LESS any payments made through the bank account. In other words Jim will transfer £194.52 to his account (£200 less the £5.48 spent on iTunes) and Alison will transfer £188.75 (£200 less the £11.25 spent on CDs). The figures will then all balance out and they will be 100% correct (and automatic) for the next month. After that, it's just a question of remembering to use the right card for the right purchase!

There are a couple of other points to mention. You may recall that Jim and Alison had quite a major overspend in January, as they almost certainly did in the months prior to that. Since this spend has all been done and we're starting afresh, it is being ignored. They still made all the payments they needed to, but they DID have to add to their credit card bills a little as we've already seen. From now on they will be sticking to the budgets and not using those credit cards so the extra balance will ultimately be taken care of naturally. This will be the same for you as well. Everything that has gone before is no longer relevant, it really is a fresh start that will bring you to a point of total control and perfect financial balance sooner or later depending on the numbers you are dealing with if – and ONLY if – you stick to the budgets each month.

Obviously, your mission here is to spend less, or equal to, the budget that is set at the beginning of the month. Just knowing this is very liberating in itself. No more do you have to worry whether you can get the shopping this week or not or whether you can afford to fill the tank up, if the spreadsheet says you can, you can. And you can keep spending without worry or guilt right up until that 'Left to spend' figure reaches zero. Of course, it's better to take it easy and spread it over the month than going crazy and having to stop abruptly part way through the month, but that's something you'll work out as you go. Once you get REALLY good at managing your spend correctly, you may even find that you have some left over near the end of the month. This is the best feeling of all – you could treat your family to a night out knowing that you can afford it and you've well

94

and truly earned it. Or, you might choose instead to keep it in your account, because anything you don't spend will automatically be added to the next month meaning even more disposable income to use as you wish.

But we have to acknowledge the other side too. If you go over budget, there will be things we need to consider. First of all, the following month will start with a downward adjustment, meaning that there is less money available. In reality, you'll never manage to spend the exact amount, so there will always be adjustments of some sort, but the trick is to keep it within a very narrow range around where it should be.

The second part to this is considering whether you will have enough money to pay everything you need to, especially if it's your first 'proper' month or you have used your emergency or savings fund. This is the only time you will need to keep a close eye on the bank account because incurring fees or penalties will only compound the problem. In all cases, it is always better to make sure you stick to the budget, or thereabouts, because the system works perfectly that way. As a reminder, the power to increase your available monthly spend lies with YOU via a combination of completing the fixed payment reductions, better planning on day to day items or even increasing income, which we'll touch on later.

From now on, either every day, or at least every couple of days, simply log in to your online banking and update the spreadsheet with your latest spend. It really does take only a couple of minutes to give you that control. When you reach the end of the month and are ready to start the next one, simply place an 'x' in the 'Start this month? (x)' section of the spreadsheet and it will do the rest for you, including making any adjustments from the previous month. All you have to do from now on is make sure you stick to your budget!

Chapter Thirteen
Changing, updating and amending

Nothing stays the same forever and as time goes by you'll need to amend some of your numbers on both the income and expenditure side to make sure the system keeps working for you. However, since you have now done all the work, any changes you make will automatically feed through and keep everything updated for you.

The first instance where you'll probably need to make some changes is when any reductions on your monthly debits start to come through and you need to amend the monthly amounts on your 'Master Account Planner (MAP)' spreadsheet. It's all designed to be straightforward though, so making any changes should be painless. That said, I always recommend having an up to date backup copy before you do change anything in case something goes wrong.

Jim and Alison, for example, had several changes they were working on and as they are confirmed by the companies they were negotiating with, they will make the changes they need to. They had already managed to cancel the mobile phone insurance (removing £8.50 a month effective from March), reduce the home insurance figure (reducing the cost to £20.54 a month effective from the renewal date in April) and combine the TV, internet and phone packages (creating a new, single cheaper cost of £53.25 a month on the 22nd of the month, effective in March also.)

On the 'Master Account Planner (MAP)' spreadsheet, it may seem simpler at first to just delete the line labelled 'Phone Insurance Company' but we can't do this because, first, it will remove figures that we have used in previous months, affecting their accuracy and, second, it is far better to leave the historical numbers in so you can see which changes you made and when and where. However, when you're setting up a new year in the future, it's ok to leave it out completely at that point if you want to.

Instead, Jim and Alison simply reduce the figure in that line to '0' from March onwards. When they start March's expenses on their 'Budget Manager' spreadsheet, it will take this change into account and amend the available spend and savings figures accordingly.

For the home insurance, all they need to do is reduce the monthly amount from £28.54 to £20.54 from April onwards, assuming that the direct debit date is the same. I always recommend this anyway, even when changing suppliers, because it means you are used to the debit occurring at a certain time of the month. Almost all suppliers now let you choose your preferred date these days, but if that's not possible you'll simply need to amend the date on the spreadsheet.

The final one is more complicated as they're changing several things, but it's still not difficult to do. The new company that will now be providing the TV, internet and home phone in one package at a cheaper combined cost of £53.25 a month is taking its direct debit on the 22nd of the month, the same day that one of the last payments was due. This means all Jim and Alison have to do is change the name of that line slightly – from 'Phone and internet package' to perhaps 'Combined TV, phone, internet' or similar – and change the amount to £53.25 a month effective from March. They must also remember to set the previous (and now redundant) 'TV Package subscription' line entries to '0' from March onwards.

By the time they have finished, their newly updated 'Master Account Planner (MAP)' spreadsheet looks like this:

NOTE: A larger, clearer version of this image is available at www.originalcryptoguy.com under 'Books by Jason'

As you can see, this has increased the available income going forward, but has not affected any of the historical data we have entered so far. Of course, as times goes by, Jim and Alison hope to make further reductions and they'll use the same system to amend any figures going forward, letting the spreadsheet do all the work in terms of making any changes elsewhere.

There's also the other side of the coin. Over time, we'd expect their income figures to change as well, perhaps at an annual review, or with a bonus, or with a change of job. Even if there was an adverse development such as a loss of a job or income, the spreadsheets will still work and let you know what you have to do to keep the numbers working and make it clear what the size of the gap to 'plug' would be.

You may remember that when we entered the figures initially on the 'Income Tracker' spreadsheet, for ease of entry they were simply averages copied across the rest of the year. In reality, it could be that your income varies a little each month – perhaps due to overtime or shift work – so we'll need to adjust it. The problem is, of course, we don't know what those changes will be exactly until we get the payslips, so we can only adjust them in 'real time'.

The next question – and one that always comes up – is which payment goes where. For example, most people are paid at the end of the month, so does January's pay go in January or February? The common sense answer is to treat the month that you're actually using the money as the month it refers to. You might get paid on 31st January, but you're really going to spend it in February, so you would enter it in February's entry instead. Some companies pay in the middle of the month and it is straightforward to allocate, but in the end it doesn't actually matter what date it comes in through the month (once you are past the first one) as long as you are sticking to the budgets all the time.

To change each month, simply overwrite the relevant number directly. For example, Jim is paid at the end of the month, so he'll enter February's net pay amount (i.e. the amount that is paid directly into the joint account) as March's income since that's when he'll really use it. He simply goes to the cell where his income is showing at £2,400 under 'March' and changes it to the amount he received for that month which, let's say, is £2,495.50 as he had to do a little overtime. This automatically adjusts the figures for March right across the spreadsheets including disposable income figures and savings, but does not change any of the historical entries. Importantly, it also doesn't adjust any of the income figures going forward as, again, we can't know exactly what these will be.

There is also a lot of scope for entering any other income on this spreadsheet. Just as we get unexpected bills and problems, we can sometimes get unexpected or extra incomes. It might be selling something off, it might be an insurance payment, a refund, a premium bond prize, a gift – literally anything at all. It doesn't really matter, we just need to account for it and by using this spreadsheet system it can be correctly allocated and made to work for us immediately. Simply enter the extra income in the month that it applies to and the other figures will automatically adjust. You can make a note of what it is if you want to by right-clicking and selecting 'insert comment.'

Remember any tax that is made on extra earnings must be declared at the end of the year, but remember also that certain things are exempt. For example, anything that you sell that you own (that isn't part of a business or was bought specifically to resell at a profit) is not usually classed as taxable income. It's worth checking out carefully and properly, and there's lots of useful information on the government's tax website at www.hmrc.gov.uk.

Incidentally, if you sold some items, for example, and got cash for it rather than a bank or PayPal payment, you have a choice to make. You could either put it in the bank and add it into your income on the spreadsheet, or you could simply use the cash next time you go shopping to reduce your overall outgoings. There's no right or wrong answer in my view and it depends how you want to track it, or even if you want to in the first place. The system will still work for you either by adding it into your disposable income figure, or by carrying forward any spare disposable income you have to the next month which might be there as a result of having a little more available.

In the meantime, as you can see, making amends to any part of the spreadsheet is very simple once you have carried out the work to set it up. If you're worried about doing something wrong, I'd suggest making regular backups, perhaps once a week in different files, until your confidence level is high enough that you can make changes without worrying. That said, I always recommend doing backups regularly, or at least keeping your information in the cloud rather than just on one machine, because having to set it all up again is a pain.

And for the future? Once you've completed the whole year, you can download the spreadsheet again and set up a new one for the next year by simply copying over the basic information. This is very easy to do as you won't need to carry out all the analysis again each time, but by all means refer to this book if you need to.

And .... Well, that's it.

I'm serious, it really is.

Remember when you started this exercise? Perhaps it seemed daunting, impossible or just far too much work, and yet you're here, officially in full control of managing your finances! You have completed the entire process and now have all the information you need to make your money work exactly how *you* want it to, rather than being pulled from pillar to post and trying to make it through the month in one piece. I have worked with many people and know what a completely liberating and exciting feeling this is. I also experienced it myself all those years ago when I realised I had to find a way to get control of my own situation.

I offer you my sincerest and fullest congratulations - a future with one less worry awaits you!

Or does it? Perhaps you still have some questions or concerns that still need answering. Perhaps having done the analysis it has only shown you how bad things are and actually *caused* more stress by forcing you to confront it. If you fall into any of these areas, the next chapter may be the one that could help you more than any other.

And even if you don't, I have a feeling you might find it interesting anyway.

Chapter Fourteen
End the financial struggle for good

Over the years of working with people in general and couples in particular, I have found that completing this process always – and I really do mean ALWAYS – leads to a better place in the end. However, for some people this may only be a step in that process, rather than the end of it. These people are normally identified as those whose debts are simply too high, or they are far too far down that slippery slope to use this process to recover.

If you believe this applies to you, then, as usual, my first piece of advice is still the same: **Don't panic, don't stress and don't give up**. There are still several routes we can take, but let's make doubly sure what we're dealing with first.

If you are in a situation where your fixed payments are leaving you with no disposable income at all or a completely unrealistic amount of disposable income, we have to get far more ruthless and we have to do it now. Like everything, we have to do this logically – not emotionally - and we can do this by looking at a series of questions.

Question One
Can you quickly - and permanently – reduce your fixed outgoings?

I don't mean in the same way as we did before, i.e. looking where we can shave a few pounds here and there to get maximum value (although we should always do that), I mean in a far more aggressive way. Think of it like this: if we could make those debits go away, would it end the stress? It's worth it, it always is, even for the short term pain.

Can you get out of that car lease? Can you dump the expensive sports and movies packages from the TV company and live without them whilst working through this recovery? What other 'luxuries' can you dump, here and now, to try and release the pressure a bit? Be ruthless, in fact, be utterly and totally ruthless. What is the absolute bare minimum you can whittle it down to? Remember again, that it is NOT forever, it is only about getting control back into your life. Once you have it, you can get some or all of these back later, if you decide you still want them.

It may be possible to get payment holidays on things like mortgages and loans, but I really have a problem with this approach if nothing else is done in the meantime. You'll almost certainly destroy your credit rating and you'll only be postposing the inevitable if the outgoings are still the same. The great thing about being able to see the rest of the year visually is that it is pretty clear where you'll be in the future. And believe me, the future has this nasty habit of becoming the present soon enough. If there are no other fundamental changes, the problem may well remain or even be more overwhelming.

Question Two
Could you survive, short term, until X, Y, Z happens?

This question is one that asks you to look at the bigger picture. Perhaps you are heavily weighed down by a huge loan repayment for now, but you can see it will end in six months' time. How realistic is it that you could survive on 'beans on toast' for that period and forgo all the other luxuries you possibly can? It sounds awful of course, but remember that this is not permanent and the spending restraint you'll learn doing this will serve you incredibly well in the future. It will also avoid more drastic action being taken by you or by your creditors. Have perspective: in a year's time, this will all be a distant memory, oft told and preceded by the line "Do you remember when we were so broke that we …" Finally, it will bring you together as you'll be united in a common cause. I can assure you it's possible to achieve, I've seen it myself many, many times.

Question Three
Can you increase your income to match your commitments?

This one has a lot of possibilities because it also depends on the two questions above and how realistic the whole situation is. If you have a short term issue, e.g. the big loan finishing soon situation, what *extraordinary* steps could you take to mitigate the situation right now? Can you sell something? Can you get extra hours at work? Can you get another part time job, even if it means sacrificing something else in the meantime? Can you do all of these things, or any others you can think of? Be creative, think out of the box. At the end of the day, if you have a financial issue with a specific end date, it's worth pulling out all the stops to get that control back. Even better, because you can see EXACTLY what effect your extra efforts are having on your financial future through the spreadsheet system, it is extremely rewarding, especially as you know – categorically – that you'll get there. But play by the rules – extra earnings must be declared. It's not worth solving the problem only to end up with a big fine – or worse – at the end of it.

Question Four
If you do all of these things, to one extent or another, is the situation still 'hopeless' in your view?

This is a big one, and we do need to be very, very clear on what 'hopeless' means. I would define it as your normal monthly income not coming close to even covering your (scaled down) fixed outgoings, let alone the disposable income element. Conversely, I have always believed that if you can cover those payments and have at least *some* disposable income left, there's usually a way to make it through. Yes, it may require a longer term concerted and consistent focus, fanatical application of the thinking offered by the previous three questions and even quite a lot of pain, but it should be possible to do, especially with this system in place showing you what's ahead. It is at least, in my view, very much worth a shot. You will, ultimately, regain full control and will be considerably wiser for the experience.

If, however, you are very definitely not able to cover the fixed element of your outgoings and you simply cannot scale them back any further, then it may be time to seek professional advice. The work you have done here will prove invaluable, as you will have a proper and detailed breakdown of the situation you are in for their consideration of how you manage it going forward. Put it this way, whilst it may not have provided the answer you were hoping for, it has given you total clarity for what you must do next. The most important thing to do now is act – even though perhaps every fibre in your body is resisting it – and the sooner the better. At least this way you are still in control of sorting it out and are not being forced into that situation by someone else. However, the longer you leave it, the less likely this is to be the case.

As scary as all this sounds, remember I am suggesting only that you seek advice at this stage to weigh up what the best options are. There are many charities and organisations that are out there to help you and I keep an up to date list of links I think are useful on my website at www.originalcryptoguy.com in the same location you were able to find the spreadsheets and other resources referred to previously. Feel free to visit this at any time and use any information there that will help. But act quickly and get that control whilst you still can.

Finally, whilst on the subject, I just want to address the issue of additional borrowing to solve the problem, usually in the form of consolidation loan. On paper, I completely understand this seems to make sense. After all, you borrow a much larger sum, usually over a longer period, and pay off all your other debts with it, leaving a single, smaller monthly payment to manage over many years. The issue I have with it is that it doesn't deal with the underlying problem which means that most people just end up where they were to start with, except this time the monthly payments are bigger than ever and consolidating again isn't possible.

Let me be clear: I'm not saying this is *definitely not* an option, I am simply drawing on years of experience where I have witnessed this being done and – mostly – the only result being that it moves the problem a few months or years down the road. Of course, I have also seen a few successful outcomes and these have come from people who have installed and then religiously followed either this or some other form of tracking system for an extended period of time. It IS possible, but the psychology is against us right at the start – when that money comes in, the problem immediately appears to go away, which means we can spend again, and then so often do. We all fall for it to some extent, so it can be a dangerous move. In short, take advice, take careful stock of your situation and be honest with yourself in how you think you would handle it before proceeding.

Whatever your next steps are, remember that the moment you start the process of gaining control, its days of controlling YOU are immediately numbered. It's much easier to start that journey, which may be hard at times, knowing that it has a definite end. If you've identified that you need that extra advice, don't hesitate.

Do it now.

Chapter Fifteen
Going for it!

If you look back at what you have done through the course of reading this book, realise that you have achieved a lot and have put in a great deal of work. Not only is it no small feat, it is the vast majority of the work you'll ever need to do in most circumstances. But whilst the next steps – whatever they are for you – may now be clear, there's still one ingredient that you'll need for it all to work:

You need <u>CONSISTENT ACTION</u>

In other words, you've set down the foundation and laid out the path, but you still need to walk that path to let it take you where it leads. It's no good pulling up a deckchair and simply admiring it – you'll still be in the same place!

Despite having completed all of this work, I have still seen a few situations where it hasn't worked for the people I've been helping. There are generally only two reasons for this, and the first of those is usually to do with the forming of new habits or the self-discipline of filling in the spreadsheets on a regular basis.

This system needs, and in fact only works on, small actions being taken on a consistent basis. First of all, it is essential that you develop a way of updating, and referring to, the spreadsheets that you are using. Doing this on a phone or tablet IS possible, but it's a bit fiddly and it's usually easier to do it on a laptop or PC. If you have a main PC at home then this is perhaps the one to set it up on and you can set shortcuts on your desktop for the spreadsheets and in your browser tab for your online banking. By doing the set up this way, it means updating is only ever a matter of a few clicks of the mouse. If you do it daily, the whole process will take 3-5 minutes from end to end, and you have a real time view of how you're doing which is essential in those 'cutting it close' months. Of course, if you're running well most of the time, then doing this update every few days is fine and actually the total time it takes is no different to do. In this case, you'd be realistically looking at 10-15 minutes a week to stay in control of your finances for good. That's entirely possible for anyone's schedule.

On its own though, that's not enough. Beware of the trap of entering the numbers and then not really looking at them, because this could still make you a passenger on the trip if you're not using the information to your advantage. For example, if you see that you're getting close to your budget limit for the month and you carry on spending as normal, the effect of doing the work is zero. The spreadsheet system gives you a very nice visual idea of what the situation is, but it's up to you to use that information to constantly tweak and adjust where you're going and what you're spending. There's a real danger that if you don't 'feel' anything is changing because you're not using the information it provides, you could still facing the same issues in a few months' time. Then, you'll gradually lose confidence in it and stop entering the data. This puts you right back where you started, firmly relieving you of the control you need.

The other danger in terms of forming habits, and probably the one that is most common, is not sharing the information with your partner. Often this is not done deliberately, i.e. by withholding the information, but by omission, i.e. where one of you is updating the spreadsheet and understanding it and the other one is simply not aware of what's going on. This can lead to all sorts of problems including the system not working at all, so the trick is to come up with a way that both of you can either look at it together, perhaps via a quick weekly catch up (which doesn't need to be anything formal), or at least passively where both of you can see where you are even if it's at different times of the day or week. I've seen all sorts of variations of this and there's no hard and fast rule - the trick is to find something that fits your routine and lifestyle. All that matters is that both partners are on the 'same page' when it comes to the monthly joint account spend.

The second reason where installations of this system have failed is purely psychological and it is almost exclusively to do with fear, and not just one type either. Over the years I've observed many different forms of fear that have manifested themselves in some way when helping people, though, in most cases they haven't used the actual words we'll be discussing below. The funny thing is that fear is very hard thing to admit to and we tend to find another reason why we can't or won't do something to hide the fact that it IS fear. There's probably all sorts of reasons for this but I'm not qualified to comment on them, suffice it to say it feels very real and almost certainly something we've all done at some point or another, myself included. The key point is that fear can be a real action killer and it's worth taking just a couple of minutes to confront the issue head on, even if you think this doesn't apply to you. Although there are many fear types, it seems to be three main types that are prevalent in this context:

Fear of Failure

This fear usually manifests itself with the following thoughts:

"What if this doesn't work?"

"What if I try it and fail – wouldn't that be worse than it is now?"

"What if I'm just not capable of doing this?"

This one can be quite nasty because it tries to prevent you from doing anything that might be new or different. It can force you to accept the status quo because, although you may not necessarily like where you are, it's familiar and 'known'. It also ties into this strange idea that we all seem to have, to some degree or another, where we tend to overestimate other people's abilities and underestimate our own. It's rarely actually the case.

My reply to this is always the same and incredibly simple: As long as you follow all the directions in this book, it WILL work and I can assure you 100% that you are entirely capable of doing this. That part is real and fact. The fear, on the other hand, is only an illusion and a leap of faith will make it disappear like the fraud it is.

Fear of Success

This one is fascinating since it makes you resistant to actually achieving something. It is usually accompanied by thoughts along these lines:

"I don't know if I'd like my life running the way this book organises it for me."

"What would I have to give up to get to the point where I have achieved that financial control?"

In other words, if you did actually succeed at doing what this book suggested, could it be the wrong choice? Would living with the results actually be worse than carrying on as you are now?

My view, biased as it is, would be that this will almost never be the case, but I'd also add that there is nothing to stop you trying it on for size and testing that fear. If you don't like it, simply dismantle it, delete the spreadsheets and carry on as you were. But try it first and see if that fear is real or imaginary. I bet I know which one it will be.

Fear of what other people think

The first two fears, whilst appearing real to some people, aren't usually enough to cause inaction once we have been through the processes outlined in this book. This last one, however, can be a real problem to many of us.

For some, even the fact that they have bought this book may not be something they want to share. It might even be the sort of book you'd be uncomfortable reading on the train, even though it could be used by anyone in almost any situation. Money, often being linked to status, is an incredibly complex social subject with all sorts of written and unwritten rules that we abide by, even though those rules may vary wildly from person to person. There is no doubt that the pressure to 'keep up with the Joneses' is a very real phenomenon for many people but even where that is not the case, just appearing to 'fit in' and 'be normal' so we can be accepted is just as important to us as humans. Sometimes this doesn't sit well with making the changes we may need to make to get to the point where you have complete control. After all, what would our peer group think?

It might seem simple for me to say something along the lines of "What's more important: what the neighbours think or the fact that you have full financial control of your life?" but the reality is that logic on its own quite often doesn't work here and you probably already know all the logical arguments anyway. At some level, we have our social position and our natural tendency to compare ourselves with others to consider. This can be a very real and a very stubborn problem to overcome and in my opinion it can be the biggest obstacle of the three main fears.

However, the fact that you are reading this book already gives you a distinct advantage, since it shows that you are already open to the idea of change or, at the very least, you recognise that change needs to be made. In my view, this fear can be overcome by using several small steps which we will examine below.

First, you don't have to tell anyone if you don't want to whilst you're getting yourself into a position of control. Simply avoid or play down money conversations when they come up while the process is ongoing. Later on, when you have control, peace of mind and a new air of confidence that people will notice (and they will, believe me) you can share, if you wish, that you made a 'few changes' some time ago and feel much happier, financially, as a result. You might be surprised by some of the comments and questions you get and it may even lead you to promote this book and system to them. It's happened before, more than once!

Second, and building on the comment I made earlier about the often incorrect assumption that other people's abilities are superior to our own, you may be extremely surprised to learn that other people's financial situations are often not what they appear to be. I have been happy to help people from all walks of life, including people who ostensibly appear very wealthy, who simply aren't and people who appear to live a very frugal lifestyle who have a surprisingly high net worth. The point is that more often than you think it's not possible to tell someone's true financial status from the outside.

Third, I like to turn the situation around to give us a more objective look. Let's say you found out your neighbours were installing this system. Would your assumption be that it's because they haven't managed their money correctly and have got themselves in trouble? Or because they are smart people who are looking to make sure they maintain full control going forward? Your relationship with them may, therefore, affect your point of view. But here's the big question: would it really matter? Would you expect them to live their lives based on what your view of the subject was? Of course not, and neither, for that matter, should you.

Finally, after completing the process in this book you may be one of the people who need to take extra advice going forward, perhaps leading to a harder short term situation. This may have the greatest level of 'what other people think' fear attached to it, yet it is also the one that comes with a greatest level of support from many people along the way. From the moment you make your first call to ask for help, you'll be quite amazed at the amount of empathy for your situation you'll receive. If this is something you have now identified that you need to do, remember, once again, that nothing lasts forever and the future is not set in stone. But act now and act quickly. You'll be taking the most positive steps possible to resolve the situation and eventually (and almost certainly sooner than you currently believe) you'll be in a position where YOU are the one in control.

In any case, by completing the work that you have done so far, you have already taken tremendous strides to take control of your financial future, so stay the course, reap the benefits... and watch that fear evaporate as you do.

Chapter Sixteen
A final word

This book is focussed on getting a system in place to help you, your partner and your family gain total control of your finances, both now and going forward. It could be that you've gone through the process because you've identified a problem, or it could be that you've been proactive and were looking for a way to keep everything under control, but either way, and for whatever your reason, it will lead you to the same place.

It may, however, also start you thinking about your lifestyle as a whole. Perhaps you'd like to earn more money and now that you know you have a solid basis with which to control it and make it work for you, this suddenly seems even more worthwhile to do. Perhaps you've identified that you will have certain funds available in the future so you would like to find ways to increase your net worth through investment, but are not yet sure how. All of these thought processes are welcome and, as a couple or as a family, you can now work together to explore them. After all, it may well be that all of these things were not real possibilities before, having been drowned out by stress and distraction.

This, of course, is beyond the scope of this book, but, once again, on my website at www.originalcryptoguy.com, under 'Books by Jason' and selecting 'MONEY: Yours, Mine or Ours?' you will find links to books I have found very helpful in my own financial adventures that I am happy to recommend to you. Many are very well known, some not so much, but in every case I attach real credibility to them. Find the areas that interest you, take your time and use all the resources at your convenience to do your research.

In the meantime, if you have found this book useful and have installed the recommended system in your household, I'd love to hear your story, if you're happy to share it with me. Simply use the contact form on the website to reach me directly.

Finally, remember that this book provides the tools and the framework. It is YOU who has done the work and it is YOU who now stands – firmly and squarely – in control of your household budget. Not the amount of month left, not any creditors who are vying for attention, and not even that nagging voice that's constantly reminding you that you're borrowing more and more each month.

Take a moment to savour that thought with your partner and wonder at the possibilities this gives you. Yes, it may seem like there's a tough month or two (or even more) ahead if you're just starting out, but the way is clear and the terms under which you'll be running your financial lives, perhaps for the first time in a long time, are yours.

And that thought alone is utterly priceless.

Welcome to perfect financial balance!